W9-ANP-588

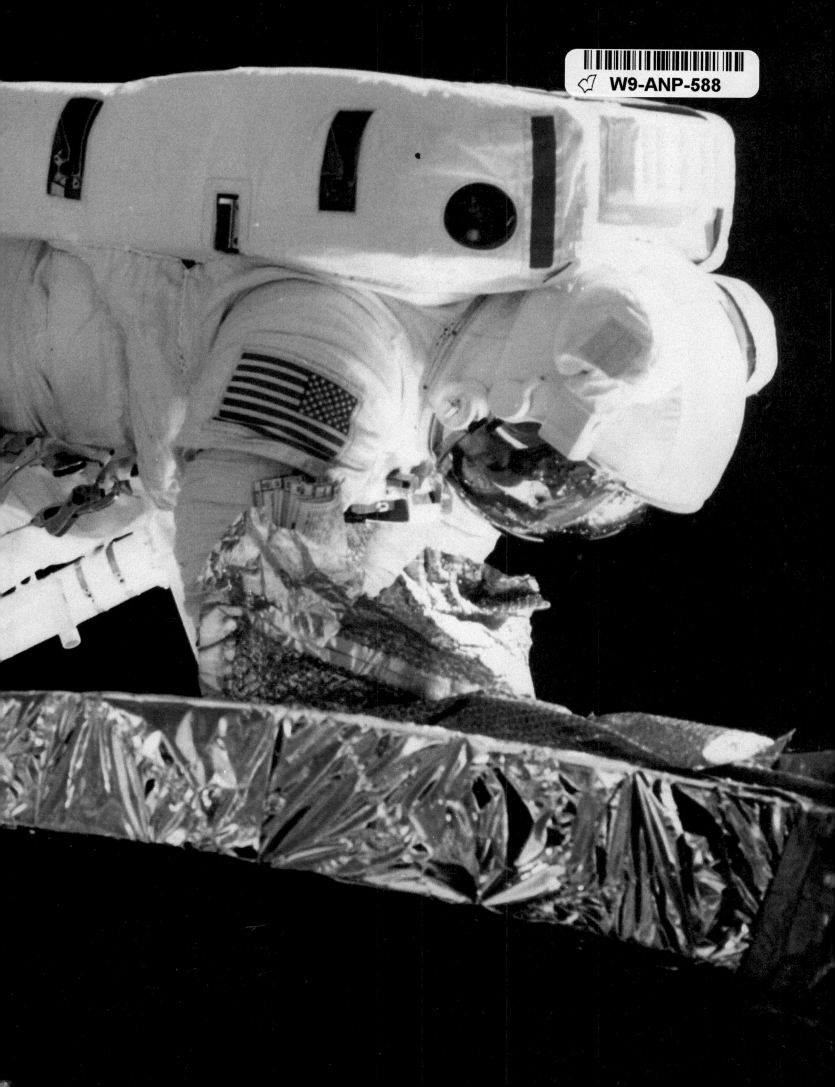

WATERLOO HIGH SCHOOL LIBRARY
1464 INDUSTRY RD.
ATWATER, OHIO 44201

LIVING IN SPACE

LIVING IN SPACE

Robin Kerrod

Crescent Books   New York

WATERLOO HIGH SCHOOL LIBRARY
1464 INDUSTRY RD.
ATWATER, OHIO 44201

This book was devised and produced by
Multimedia Publications (UK) Ltd

Editors: Jeff Groman and Tony Hall
Production: Karen Bromley
Design: Mick Hodson
Picture Research: Spacecharts. Thanks are
also due to the Threshold Corporation,
a subsidiary of Imax Systems Corporation,
which supplied pictures on pages 52-53.

Copyright © Multimedia Publications (UK) Ltd 1986

All rights reserved. No part of this book may be
reproduced or transmitted in any form or by any means,
electronic or mechanical, including photocopying and
recording, or by any information storage retrieval
system, without permission in writing from the
publisher and the copyright holders.

1986 edition first published in the United States,
by Crescent Books, distributed by Crown Publishers, Inc.

ISBN 0 517 60602 X

Typeset by Rowland Phototypesetting (London) Limited
Origination by Scan Studios Limited
Printed by Cayfosa, Barcelona, Spain
Dep. Leg. B-20.081-1986

Contents

Introduction

It is now more than 25 years since a Soviet Air Force Lieutenant named Yuri Gagarin blazed the human trail into space. On 12 April 1961 powerful rockets ignited beneath him and blasted him into the heavens. Within minutes he was traveling ten times faster than any human being before him through the deadliest environment man has ever encountered: through a high vacuum to which even fleeting exposure spells death; where cosmic radiation can be lethal; where temperatures are either scorching hot or deathly cold.

Could this being of flesh and blood even survive the terrifying forces unleashed by the rockets that threatened to crush the life out of him as he soared skyward? Could he later survive similar forces when he re-entered the Earth's atmosphere on his return? And could he in-between tolerate the unique weightlessness of orbit when the brain becomes disorientated and the body organs float free? Could he still eat, drink, remain rational and control his actions? He could, and he did.

In the month following Gagarin's flight, Alan Shepard became the first American astronaut, making a successful suborbital flight in a Mercury capsule. Early in 1962 Mercury astronaut John Glenn sped three times around the Earth to become the first American in orbit. Slowly but surely human beings began invading outer space.

In the United States the one-man Mercury flights gave way to the two-man Gemini missions, each accumulating data and experience which suggested that, as long as they were given the hardware, human beings could survive and even enjoy the rigors of space flight with no ill-effects — at least for periods of up to two weeks.

Gemini in turn paved the way for Apollo and the greatest adventure in the history of the world, the attempt to land a man on the Moon before the decade of the 1960s was out. And the goal was achieved, not once, but twice in 1969. Neil Armstrong's 'small step' when he planted his footprint on the Moon's ancient dusty surface on 20 July 1969, marked mankind's great leap into interplanetary space.

The triumphs of Apollo behind them, American space scientists embarked on the Skylab project that was to realize the benefits of a long-term presence in space. For periods of up to two and a half months, Skylab astronauts demonstrated beyond all doubt that human beings can live and work effectively in a weightless environment without ill-effect. They also demonstrated how they could make do and mend when equipment was damaged or failed in orbit.

From the wasteful 'throwaway' technology that spawned the early space programs, there came in 1981 a quantum leap to the reusable technology of the space shuttle. This remarkable space plane took to the heavens 20 years to the day after Gagarin's trailblazing mission into the unknown. As shuttle orbiter *Columbia* first climbed into the blue Florida skies, a new era dawned that was to lead to space flight becoming an altogether more routine experience. Astronauts could now begin to show how versatile they really are, jetting about in orbit, repairing a satellite here, recovering one there, acquiring the skills in structural assembly work that they will need when in the next decade they start building the NASA space station, which could provide the springboard to yet more challenging endeavors.

The dangers inherent in space flight are, however, ever present and always will be. The *Challenger* disaster in January 1986 brought this home to people who had perhaps become too used to success. The astronauts, however, never underestimate the dangers in what they do. "Sometimes when we reach for the stars," said President Reagan at the Houston memorial service for *Challenger*'s crew, "we fall short. But we must press on despite the pain." Man will continue to probe the space frontier.

Orbiter *Challenger* leaves the confines of Earth for the fourth time as it thunders from the launch pad at the Kennedy Space Center in February 1984. One of the crew on this mission is Bruce McCandless, who will make the first untethered spacewalk. Less than two years later *Challenger* is no more, being blasted apart by a catastrophic explosion just after lift-off that kills the crew of seven and grounds the shuttle fleet.

The Hazards of Space Flight

Most of the world's population lives within about a mile (1.6 km) of sea level, where the atmosphere presses down with a force of some 14.7 pounds on every square inch (1 kg per square cm) of our body. There is oxygen in the air which enables us to breathe and stay alive.

The layer of air above us performs two other vital functions. It acts like a blanket to insulate the Earth at night and prevents too much of the heat accumulated during the day from escaping back into space. Further, it acts as a filter to block harmful radiation coming from space, particularly the ultraviolet radiation coming from the Sun — this is blocked by a layer of ozone in the upper atmosphere.

As we climb higher and higher through the atmosphere, we notice changes occurring. Its pressure gradually decreases — it becomes thinner — and there is less oxygen for us to breathe. By the time we reach the height of Everest at about 5½ miles (8.8 km) above sea level, we can hardly breathe at all. At double this altitude, at the height the supersonic airliner Concorde flies, the pressure is so low that our blood would start to boil, and the temperature is as low as $-49°F$ ($-45°$ C).

The pressure of the atmosphere continues to drop until at about 50 miles (80 km) high there is scarcely any air at all. We are almost, but not quite in space. Incidentally, anyone who flies higher than 50 miles (80 km) attains astronaut status. Eight pilots of the X-15 rocket plane, which flew between 1959 and 1969, attained astronaut status in this way.

There is no neat dividing line between the atmosphere and space; the atmosphere just tails off into nothing. Even at an altitude of 200 miles (300 km) and beyond, there are faint traces. Spacecraft that fly at such heights are eventually affected and slowed down so that they in time succumb to Earth's gravity and fall from orbit. But for all intents and purposes, at 200 miles (300 km) high, a typical altitude for the space shuttle, we are in space.

Life support

If human beings are to survive in the deadly environment that is space, they must surround

Gemini 4 astronaut Edward White drifts out of his space capsule in June 1965 to make the first American spacewalk, or EVA. He returns after more than 20 minutes, saying that the experience "must be worth a million dollars."

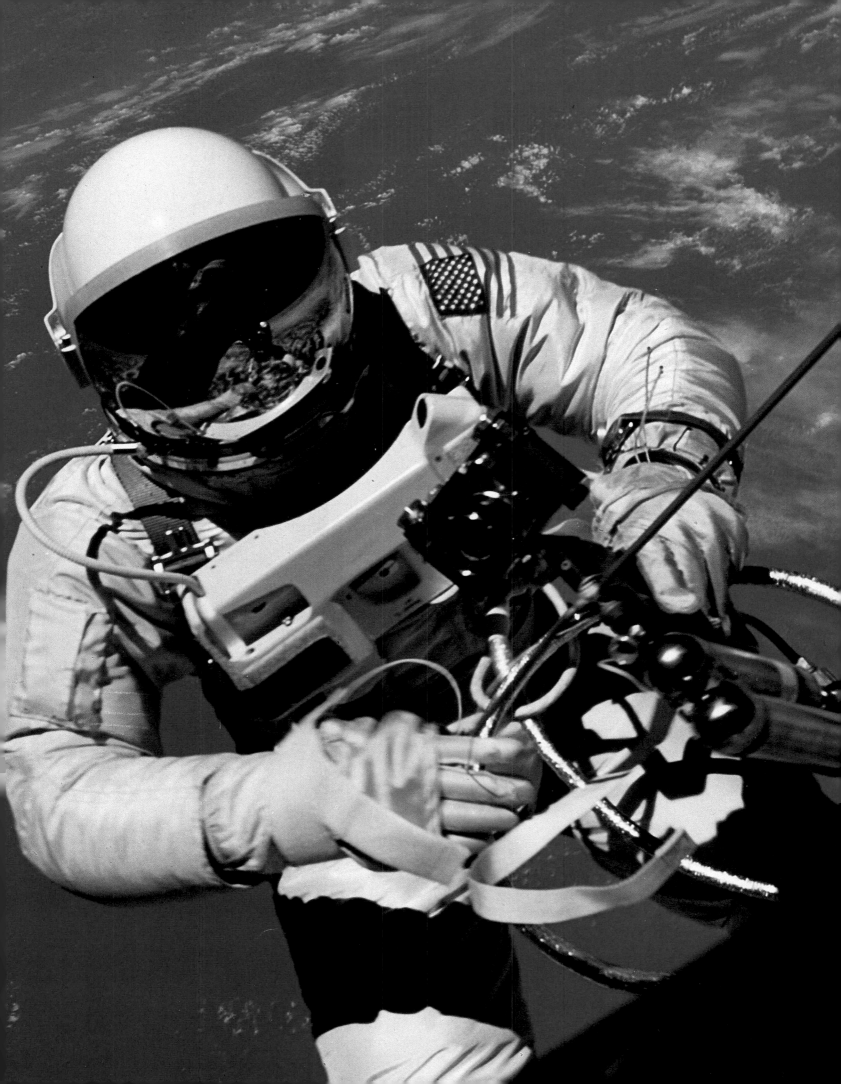

themselves with something that duplicates the various vital functions of the Earth's atmosphere. In a spacecraft, protection against radiation is afforded by the metal walls, which also guard against bombardment by the tiny dust particles, or micrometeoroids, that permeate space. A pressurized artificial atmosphere containing oxygen is provided by a life-support system. This system also removes exhaled carbon dioxide and odors and adjusts the temperature and humidity to comfortable levels.

When astronauts leave the protection of their spacecraft and go spacewalking, or perform EVA (extravehicular activity), they must be adequately protected and provided with life-support, either from their spacecraft or from a self-contained system. Protection is afforded by a spacesuit. This is a multilayer garment that insulates the astronaut from the space environment. Early American spacesuits were supplied with oxygen through an 'umbilical' tube from the on-board life-support system.

The latest shuttle spacesuit is self-contained, having a life-support backpack built-in. This supplies the oxygen for breathing and for applying pressure to the body (usually at about 4 pounds per square inch, 0.3 kg per square cm). The backpack also supplies electrical power, and cooling water for the astronaut's liquid-cooling undergarment, necessary to remove body heat while the astronaut is working.

Problems with g-forces

The provision of life support is perhaps the easiest of the space-flight problems to deal with. Much more serious problems arise when astronauts are launched into space and when they re-enter the atmosphere as they return from space. At launch, their bodies are subjected to high acceleration forces as the launching vehicle

Below
Nine years before he became one of the most famous people in history, Neil Armstrong poses in front of the X-15 rocket plane which took American pilots to the brink of space. His flying suit is similar to that worn by the early Mercury astronauts.

Right
On the pioneering moonwalk in July 1969, Neil Armstrong's colleague Edwin Aldrin is pictured in front of the Apollo 11 lunar module, having just deployed an experiment for detecting the solar wind. His multilayer spacesuit with life-support backpack protects him from the hostile lunar environment.

Left
Beneath the shuttle spacesuit astronauts wear this liquid cooling and ventilation garment, otherwise known as 'long johns'. This maintains their body at a comfortable temperature during EVA.

Right
Jack Lousma practices getting into a spacesuit in simulated zero-g inside an arcing aircraft. He has first put on the trousers of the suit and is floating up into the torso. The bands that seal the two halves of the suit are clearly seen. Notice his cooling and ventilation garment through the gap in the suit.

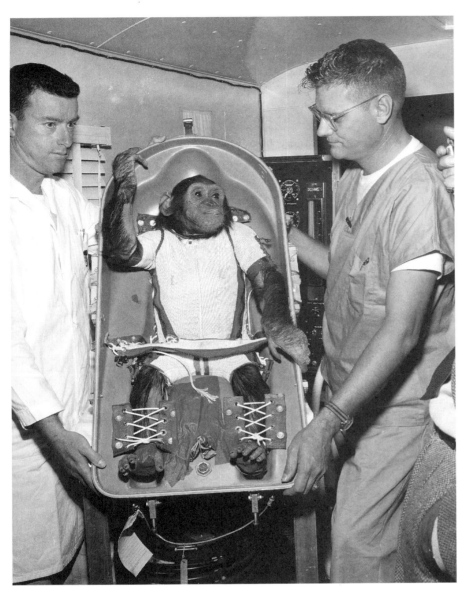

Among the animals that preceded humans into space is chimpanzee Ham. Here Ham is seen in training for his mission, which takes place in January 1961. On the flight he is launched in a suborbital trajectory in a Mercury capsule, spending 16 minutes aloft.

1962). The animal flights, though they did not always go according to plan, revealed that organisms could tolerate quite high g-forces without suffering any permanent ill-effects. These findings were confirmed when human beings followed them into space.

The main thing an accelerating or decelerating astronaut must avoid is a blackout. This occurs when, under stressful g-forces, blood drains rapidly away from the brain, causing temporary unconsciousness. If astronauts are launched with their bodies vertical, then the heart may not be able to pump blood to the brain against the g-forces, resulting in possible blackouts. They can avoid this, however, by lying horizontally. Then the heart does not have such a struggle, and blood can be pumped through the body, and particularly to the brain, far more easily. So astronauts fly into space in a 'back-down' position.

A similar argument holds for the deceleration forces on re-entry. But the astronauts on the shuttle, for instance, cannot return in the back-down position — they come back more or less feet first, the worst possible position. Even though the re-entry forces are usually less than 2g, they would be enough to cause 'grayout' (partial loss of consciousness) if not total blackout. To prevent this happening shuttle astronauts wear a special anti-g suit, which consists of trousers that inflate and apply pressure to the lower half of the body. This prevents the blood draining away from the upper half.

A weightless world

When astronauts reach orbit after their furious ascent, their bodies experience an abrupt change, from high-gs to zero-g. In orbit they and their spacecraft are in a state of 'free fall'; falling around the Earth. There is no apparent gravitational pull on their bodies, and they seem weightless. In practice, things in orbit do have a very slight weight, and 'microgravity' is the correct term for this phenomenon. Most people, however, still call it zero-g or weightlessness.

Weightlessness dominates life in orbit, dictating the way astronauts move, eat, drink, sleep, go to the toilet, and so on. They cannot, for example, walk about in the ordinary way for there is nothing to keep their feet pressed down. They have to push and pull themselves along, remembering, however, that although they have no weight they still have mass and inertia. They can also use their weightlessness to perform incredible feats of gymnastics, which can be diverting and great fun.

The weightless environment also affects the

blasts off into space. In the early days of space flight astronauts experienced forces up to seven times the pull of the Earth's gravity (7g). They also experienced deceleration forces of up to 14g, caused by the rapid braking effect of the atmosphere during re-entry.

Long before any human beings ventured into space, scientists conducted rocket tests with animals to see whether flesh and blood could withstand such high g-forces. Russian researchers used dogs in their experiments, which culminated in the flight of space dog Laika in Sputnik 2 in November 1957. American scientists on the other hand used mice, monkeys and chimpanzees.

Successful flights in Mercury capsules by astrochimps Ham and Enos preceded the first US suborbital flight by Alan Shepard (May 1961) and the first US orbital flight by John Glenn (February

body in many other ways, some good, some bad. Astronauts short of stature and carrying a little extra weight will appreciate zero-g. To begin with, the vertebrae in the spine, unaffected by gravity, begin to float apart, increasing a person's height by perhaps as much as 2 inches (5 cm). As well as this, the waistline reduces as blood, normally drawn by gravity to the lower part of the body, redistributes itself more evenly. Also the face becomes fuller, and astronauts feel literally 'swollen-headed'.

The pooling of blood in the upper body fools the brain into thinking that the body now has too much blood. This leads to the body eliminating more fluid than usual to restore the status quo, and a steady weight loss ensues.

Sickness in orbit

The initial impact of weightlessness on the body can be quite debilitating, causing violent motion sickness. Between 40 and 50 percent of astronauts experience nausea, headaches, sweating, and vomiting during the first few days in orbit. Often referred to as space sickness, this effect is correctly termed space adaptation syndrome (SAS).

The unpleasant state of SAS is caused by the body's fight to come to terms with the novel experience of weightlessness. The brain seemingly cannot cope with the conflicting messages it receives from the eyes and the balance organs in the inner ear. The body eventually adapts to the new conditions after a few days, but on short flights, like those of the shuttle, this represents a serious loss of working time.

In zero-g the heart has an easier pumping job than usual, especially when the blood volume reduces as a reaction to pooling in the upper body. As a consequence the heart begins literally to shrink in size, by as much as 10 percent on a long flight. This effect, known as cardiovascular deconditioning, can result in lightheadedness and even fainting when the body is re-exposed to gravity on returning to Earth.

Another worrying consequence of orbital flight is what is often termed space anemia. This is a progressive loss of red blood cells, perhaps as high as 15 percent. Even more serious is the reduction in the mass and strength of the bones, particularly the load-bearing bones, due mainly to a loss of calcium.

The 'bird-legs' effect

The other major problem experienced in prolonged weightlessness is the wasting away of

the muscles, particularly the calf muscles in the legs, which have little use in orbit. This muscular atrophy produces an effect known as 'bird-legs'. The legs, which slim down anyway on entering orbit because of blood redistribution, become progressively thinner as time goes by. This muscle loss bodes ill for the astronauts on their return to Earth.

Cosmonaut Yuri Gagarin pioneered manned space flight when he made one orbit of the Earth in a Vostok capsule on 12 April 1961. In 108 minutes he traveled more than 25,000 miles (40,000 km), reaching an altitude of more than 200 miles (300 km).

President John Kennedy presents NASA's Distinguished Service Medal to the first American astronaut, Alan Shepard, shortly after Shepard had made a 15-minute suborbital flight on 5 May 1961.

John Glenn needs a helping hand as he slides himself into the small interior of his Mercury capsule *Friendship 7*. It is late January 1962. The countdown will soon be starting for the launch of the first American in orbit.

Some 200 miles (300 km) off the coast of Puerto Rico, Glenn is lowered to the deck of the recovery ship USS *Noa* after his historic journey into space.

In June 1963 Russian cosmonaut Valentina Tereshkova becomes the first woman to go into space. There will not be another for 19 years. Here she is seen in London, accepting the British Interplanetary Society's gold medal from the president, L. R. Shepherd.

Right
Shooting into the blue Florida skies goes the Mercury-Atlas rocket with John Glenn on board, on 20 February 1962. Within minutes Glenn begins the first of three orbits of the Earth, which will take him nearly five hours.

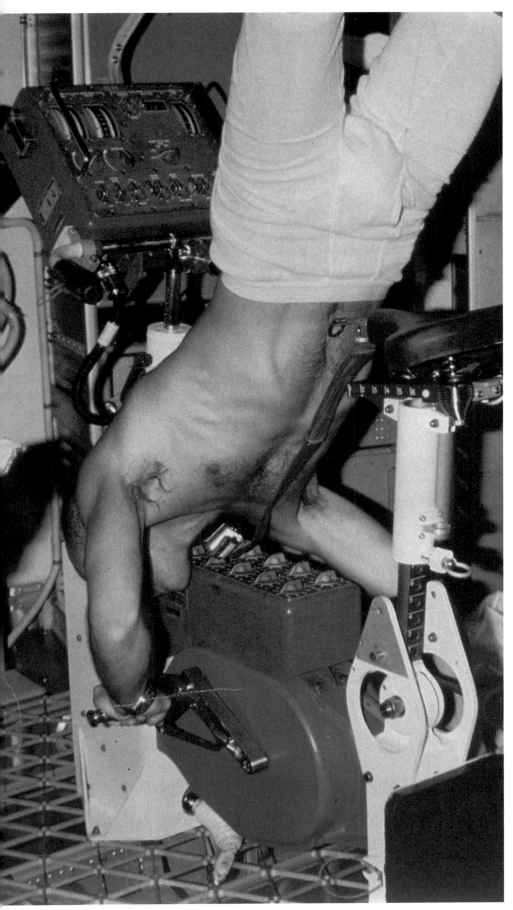

To a certain extent this wasting can be counteracted by taking regular vigorous exercise on bicycle machines and treadmills. And on long-stay missions, such as those that have taken place on Skylab and Salyut, exercise was considered an essential daily activity, as it will be on the forthcoming NASA space station. The Soviet cosmonauts on Salyut also routinely wear special 'penguin suits' that exert slight pressure on the muscles all the time.

Regular exercise and the use of special suits, however, only provide a partial solution to the problem. The cosmonauts who have spent the longest times in orbit in Salyut 7 — for 211 days and 237 days — returned to Earth with muscles so flabby that they could hardly walk for a week. Cosmonaut Valery Ryumin, who has himself spent two marathon periods of five and six months in orbit, reckons that this is too long and that four months should be the limit for a space flight, given the present state of knowledge. NASA is envisaging a maximum stay time in their space station of about three months.

The good news about the physiological deteriorations that set in during space flight is that they appear to be only temporary. The body makes good its losses after a few days, weeks or months, depending on the length of time the astronaut has been exposed to weightlessness. Some space doctors even reckon that weightlessness may indeed increase longevity, citing the example of 'monkeynaut' Baker.

Miss Baker, a squirrel monkey, was one of the animal trailblazers of the American space program, flying 300 miles (500 km) into space in 1959. On return to Earth, very much alive and kicking, she lived the life of a celebrity, appearing regularly on TV until her 'retirement' to the Alabama Space and Rocket Center at Huntsville, Alabama. She eventually died there in 1984 at the ripe old age of 27, surviving three times as long as most members of her species in captivity.

On the first manned mission to Skylab, Charles Conrad gets some exercise on the bicycle ergometer in a rather novel way. Regular exercise on the Skylab missions is to play a vital role in combating the muscle wastage weightlessness causes.

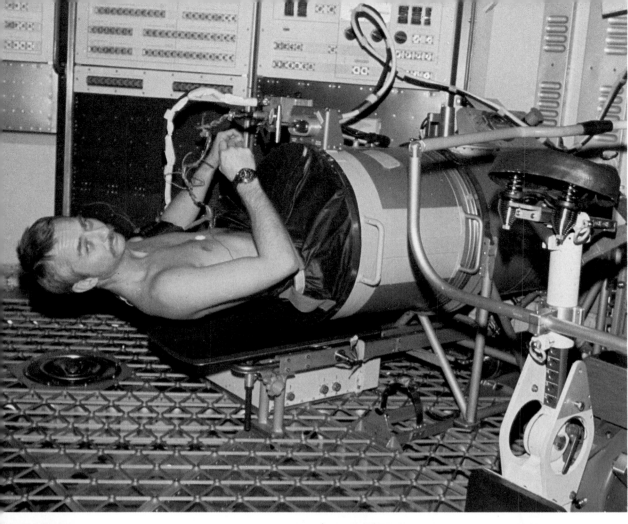

Skylab astronaut Owen Garriott taking part in an experiment to remedy some of the cardio-vascular problems that zero-g causes. In this device the lower part of the body is subjected to low pressure.

Who is upside-down in this picture taken in Soyuz's orbital module during the Apollo-Soyuz Test Project in July 1975? The answer is no-one, because there is no 'up' or 'down' in space. At the top of the picture are US astronauts Donald 'Deke' Slayton and Tom Stafford, while below is Russian cosmonaut Alexei Leonov, who ten years earlier had made the first spacewalk.

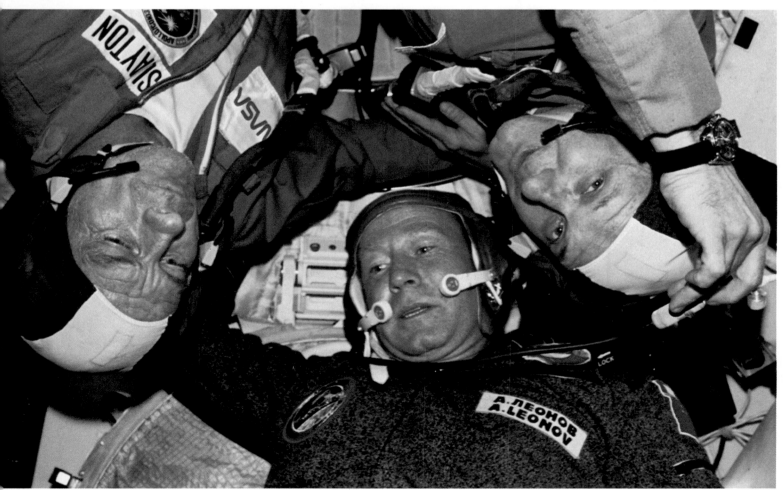

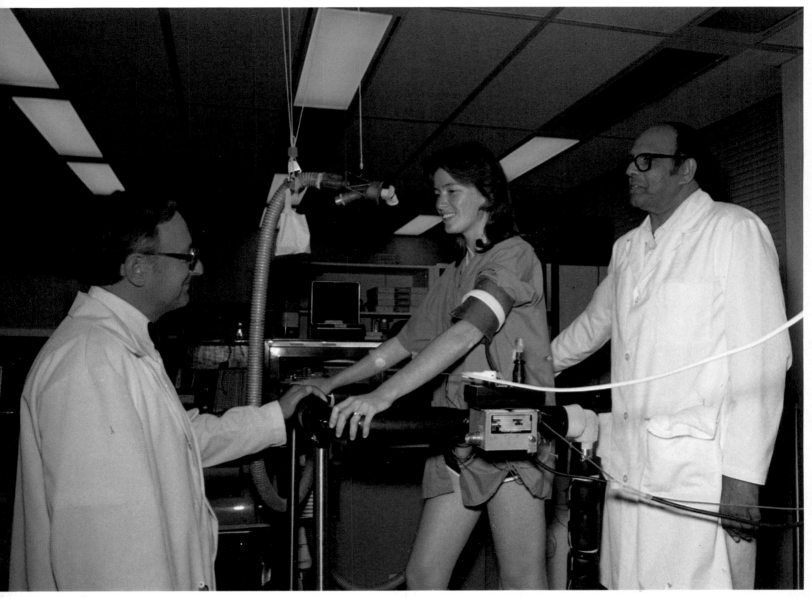

Astronauts regularly have physical checks to monitor any changes that may occur as a result of space flight. Here one of the first woman astronauts, Anna Fisher, is being put through her paces on a treadmill machine in the cardio-pulmonary laboratory at the Johnson Space Center, Houston.

Right above
Back on *terra firma* for the first time for 237 days, on 2 October 1984, are Russian cosmonauts (from the left) Leonid Kizim, Vladimir Solovyov and Oleg Atkov. They are in need of the chairs because after so long in weightless conditions their leg muscles can hardly support their body weight. Note their blackened re-entry capsule in the background.

Right below
Still spritely in 1981 is monkeynaut Miss Baker, pictured in her cage at the Alabama Space and Rocket Center at Huntsville, Alabama. She flew into space in 1959.

Training for Space Flight

Are you between 5 ft 4 inches and 6 ft 4 inches (162 and 193 cm) tall? Have you flown at least 1000 hours as pilot in command of a high-performance jet aircraft? Do you have 20/20 vision? Is your blood pressure less than 140/90 when sitting? Do you hold a bachelor's degree in engineering, science or mathematics?

If you can answer 'Yes' to each of these questions, then you stand a chance of becoming a pilot-astronaut and flying the space shuttle into orbit. You still have the chance of becoming a professional astronaut even if you are only 5 ft (152 cm) tall and have no flight experience. But you must have an outstanding scientific background, preferably with an advanced degree and related experience. You could then be considered for a mission-specialist astronaut.

And if you are a little long in the tooth, don't let this put you off. By early 1986 more than 15 operational astronauts were over 50 years old. and astronaut Karl Henize was no less than 58 when he made his first flight into space in 1985!

Recruiting the few

Not surprisingly there has never been a shortage of candidates for training as astronauts. In 1959 NASA asked the US military services to suggest personnel who could be trained for the upcoming manned spaceflight program which was about to begin. They were required to have an engineering degree and be jet pilots with test-pilot experience and with a total of at least 1500 hours flying time. They also had to be less than 5 ft 11 inches (180 cm) so that they could fit inside the cramped cabin of the Mercury space capsule.

More than 500 men from the Navy, Air Force and Marines were put forward who satisfied the initial requirements. After detailed scrutiny of their military and medical records, and stringent medical and psychological tests, the hundreds were gradually whittled down to just seven — the so-called Original Seven.

In April 1959 NASA announced their names: Navy Lieutenant Commanders Walter Schirra and Alan Shepard; Navy Lieutenant Scott Carpenter; Air Force Captains Gordon Cooper, Virgil 'Gus' Grissom and Donald 'Deke' Slayton; and Marine Lieutenant Colonel John Glenn. Alan Shepard blazed the American trail into space, though not into orbit, which honor fell to John Glenn.

As the Mercury program gave way to Gemini and Apollo, the requirements for astronaut

Training in full-size mockups occupies much of the astronauts' time. Here mission specialist Anna Fisher familiarizes herself with the shuttle orbiter flight deck in the 1g trainer at the Johnson Space Center. She is attired in the constant-wear garment she will wear in orbit.

Above
The 'Original Seven'
American astronauts are
pictured in March 1961 in
front of one of the aircraft
they fly, an F-102. From
left to right they are: Scott
Carpenter, Gordon
Cooper, John Glenn,
Virgil Grissom, Walter
Schirra, Alan Shepard and
Donald Slayton.

Right
Another astronaut in the making? A space-struck youngster samples simulated lunar gravity at the Alabama Space and Rocket Center's popular Space Camp.

Left
The astronaut intake for 1978 included these six women, the first to participate in the American space program. They have all since flown into space. From left to right they are: Rhea Seddon (who first flew on mission 51-D in 1985); Kathryn Sullivan (41-G, 1984); Judy Resnik (41-D, 1984, but who was tragically killed in the *Challenger* explosion of 1986 on mission 51-L); pioneer US woman astronaut Sally Ride (STS-7, 1983); Anna Fisher (51-A, 1984); and Shannon Lucid (51-G, 1985).

WATERLOO HIGH SCHOOL LIBRARY
1464 INDUSTRY RD.
ATWATER, OHIO 44201

Getting ready to leave the ground during parasail training is Anna Fisher, taking part in astronaut survival training in Oklahoma. This training prepares astronauts for ejection from aircraft during training flights.

Rhea Seddon stoically puts up with being dragged through the waters of Biscayne Bay as part of her survival training at Homestead Air Force Base, Florida. This particular phase of training is called 'drop and drag'.

selection became less stringent. The emphasis began to shift away from flight experience toward academic background and qualifications. A new breed of scientist-astronauts, as opposed to pilot-astronauts, was evolving. By mid-1969 a total of 73 astronauts had been selected, though many of this number had by this time resigned or had unfortunately died in accidents.

The shuttle develops

After the successful US/Soviet Apollo-Soyuz Test Project (ASTP) mission of 1975, there was a gap of six years before the next Americans flew into space. The ASTP flight marked the end of an era in US space flight — the era of expendable rocketry for propelling human beings into orbit. Henceforth astronauts would ride the shuttle into space, a reusable rocket-cum-spacecraft-cum-airplane that promised to make space flight a routine, twice-a-month event. With the prospect of up to 25 shuttle flights a year, each carrying a crew of as many as eight astronauts, NASA required a significant boost to its astronaut corps.

From the biological point of view, the shuttle was to be an altogether more user-friendly machine than the expendable 'steam-age' launching rockets, typified by the giant Saturn V Moon rocket that had powered Apollo. It would also impose much less strain on the human body during lift-off. This was reflected in less demanding physical requirements and training for astronaut candidates.

In early 1978 no fewer than 35 astronaut candidates were chosen for rigorous training and evaluation at the Johnson Space Center at Houston, the main astronaut training center. In the summer of 1979 they achieved the status of astronauts. There were 15 pilot-astronauts and 20 mission-specialists, of whom 6 were women, the first to be selected for space flight in the United States. Fourteen of the astronauts were civilians, the rest military officers.

Further astronauts were recruited in 1980 (19, including 2 women) and 1984 (17, including 3 women). The 1984 intake pattern was typical. NASA received 4934 applications from budding astronauts with the requisite qualifications. Of these only 128 were interviewed and given medical examinations at the Johnson Space Center; of these 111 went home disappointed.

One of the new breed of occasional, rather than career astronauts, is Charles Walker. Here he is seen working with biological samples when, as payload specialist, he flies on shuttle mission 41-D.

The astronauts also use the brief periods of weightlessness in the zero-g aircraft to practice getting into spacesuits and testing items of equipment. The astronaut here is Gordon Fullerton.

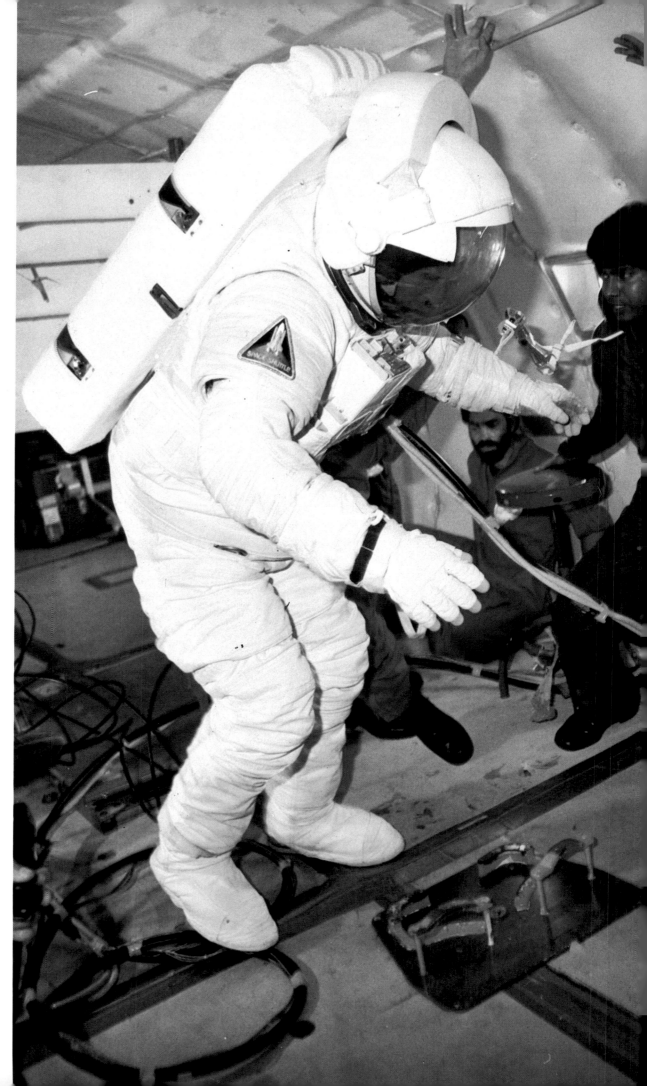

NASA reviews the size of the astronaut corps each year with specific reference to its expected work load and recruits more candidates accordingly.

The specialists

As mentioned earlier, two specific classes of professional astronaut are being recruited for shuttle flights — pilot-astronauts and mission-specialists. The former's primary responsibility is to fly the shuttle. Two pilot-astronauts are required for each flight, commander and pilot.

In addition there are usually three or more mission-specialists on board. These astronauts are concerned with the deployment of satellites and other payload operations. They are trained for extravehicular activity (EVA) and are skilled in the operation of the shuttle orbiter's remote manipulator arm in support of payload operations or EVA. They have to be familiar with all spacecraft and payload systems but do not need to know how to fly the shuttle. General shuttle 'housekeeping' is also their responsibility.

There is a third category of shuttle travelers who are not career astronauts like the pilots and mission-specialists, these are the payload-specialists. They do not need to know anything much about flying the shuttle or operating its systems. Their only concern is with a particular payload or experiment on board a particular mission. Payload-specialists are most often scientists or engineers possessing specialist skills that will be invaluable in space to help insure specific mission objectives. They will probably fly into space only once. Thanks to the relatively mild conditions experienced on board the shuttle during launch and re-entry, no long periods of conditioning is needed before they fly. A few months training will suffice.

Shuttle mission 61-B in November 1985 had a typical crew mix. The orbiter, *Atlantis*, was flown by commander Brewster Shaw and pilot Bryan O'Connor. Mission-specialists were Mary Cleave, Sherwood 'Woody' Spring and Jerry Ross. Spring and Ross's main work on the mission was to practice assembling space structures known as EASE and ACCESS in the shuttle payload bay. This they did with spectacular success, assisted from inside by Cleave, who operated the manipulator arm. From inside, Spring and Ross were also responsible for deploying three communications satellites, one (Morelos) destined for use by Mexico.

NASA has a policy of offering a payload-specialist place to customers whose payloads they carry. On this occasion they included the Mexican Rudolfo Neri Vela, and a McDonnell-Douglas scientist Charles Walker. Walker was, unusually for a payload-specialist, making his third space flight, supervising the operation of a company payload concerned with the separation of biological materials.

Ordinary guys

Occasionally NASA also offers a place on board the shuttle to someone with an expertise seemingly unrelated to specific mission requirements. We need no guesses perhaps as to why US Republican Senator Jake Garn was chosen to fly on mission 51-D in April 1985. He was chairman of a committee that holds NASA's purse strings! The political scales were balanced by Democratic Congressman Bill Nelson's flight on 61-C in January 1986. Both were described as payload-specialists and participated in on-board experiments.

To spearhead their Space Flight Participation

This is the centrifuge at Johnson Space Center, in which astronauts are whirled round at high speed to simulate the g-forces they will experience when blasting off into space. The gondola can hold a crew of three at once and was first used for training the Apollo astronauts, who flew into space three by three.

Having fun together in the zero-g environment of an arcing KC-135 aircraft are the husband and wife astronauts Anna and William Fisher. Anna joined the astronaut corps before her husband and preceded him into space.

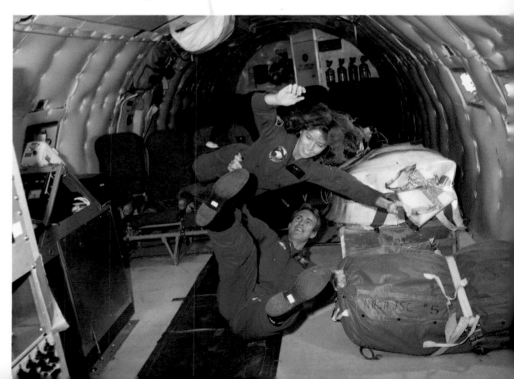

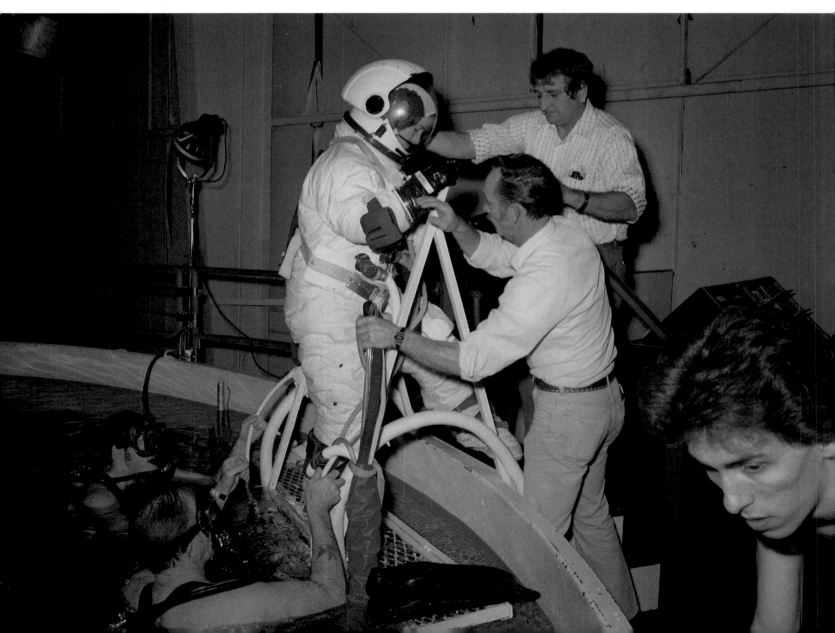

Left
Pilot-astronauts keep in
practice by flying jets like
the T-38, which also
provides their transport
between training centers.
Mission-specialists take a
back seat, coming along
for the ride.

Program, designed to expand shuttle
opportunities to a wider segment of private
citizens, NASA chose the Teacher-in-Space
project. It invited applications from American
teachers to compete for a place on mission 51-L
early in 1986. The winner would conduct lessons
live from orbit to the nation's schoolchildren.
Christa McAuliffe, from Concord, New
Hampshire, beat off competition from more than
11,000 other teachers from the 50 states and US
schools overseas.

Tragically Christa never made it into orbit,
losing her life with the other six crew when
Challenger exploded seconds after take-off on 28
January 1986. But NASA announced that the

Teacher-in-Space project would continue when
shuttle flights resumed, and Christa's backup,
Barbara Morgan, would take over the lead role.

When the disaster occurred, the deadline had
just closed on applications for NASA's Journalist-
in-Space project. The selected winner would
follow Barbara Morgan into space as the nation's
second private citizen and hopefully convey to
everyone the essence and substance of space
flight as never before.

Basic training

The main training base for shuttle astronauts is at
the Johnson Space Center at Houston. Further
training takes place at the shuttle launch site at the

Right
Inside the gigantic water
tank at the Marshall Space
Flight Center, astronauts,
assisted by divers,
practice EVA techniques
on a full-scale mock-up of
the space telescope.

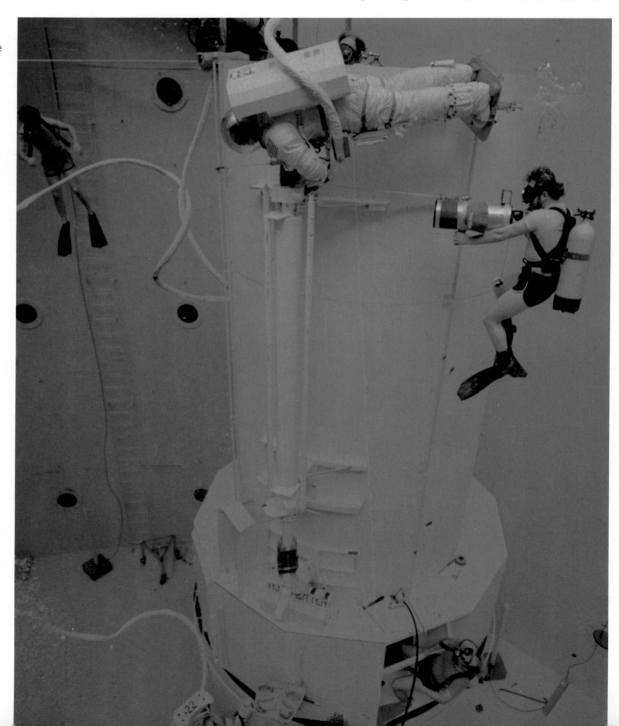

Left
Descending into the
water immersion facility
at Johnson is astronaut
Anna Fisher. Under the
water in her weighted
suit, she will experience
conditions of neutral
buoyancy that
approximate to
weightlessness.

This machine is one of the most important training aids for the pilot-astronauts. It is the shuttle mission simulator at Johnson. Inside there is a mock-up of the orbiter cockpit with instruments and controls given 'live' responses by computers.

Kennedy Space Center. The training the career astronauts receive can be broken down into various categories. They all 'go back to school' for part of the time to study disciplines relevant to space flight, such as mathematics, navigation, astronomy, physics and computers. They also undergo regular briefings on spacecraft, payloads and launch vehicle design, and the continuing modifications that are made to them. Because of the complexities of the space program, astronauts are each assigned specific areas to study and are responsible for updating the other astronauts on developments in their area.

The astronauts also train to familiarize themselves with the weightless environment that exists in orbit. They can do this briefly while flying in an aircraft. Zero-g is simulated when the aircraft flies in a parabolic trajectory up and 'over the top', climbing and descending at a 45° angle. For about 20-30 seconds at the top of the parabola, the astronauts inside the plane appear weightless. Then they practice such activities as

eating, drinking, putting on spacesuits and using equipment. NASA uses a KC-135 jet aircraft for this job.

Astronauts can experience longer periods of simulated weightlessness in a huge water tank, known as a neutral buoyancy simulator or water immersion facility (WIF). NASA's original WIF is located at the Marshall Space Flight Center at Huntsville, Alabama. Over 80 ft (25 meters) in diameter and 40 ft (13 meters) deep, it holds nearly 1½ million gallons (5.3 million liters) of water. There is now a smaller WIF at Johnson.

Inside the WIF, astronauts wear modified spacesuits, weighted so that they neither sink nor rise — they are in a state of neutral buoyancy. It is as close as they can get to the weightlessness they will experience in orbit. Inside the WIF they practice their EVA routines, working on realistic and full-size mock-ups of, typically, the shuttle's orbiter payload bay and payloads.

The pilot-astronauts keep in practice by flying high-speed jets like the T-38. Mission specialists go along too in the back seat. They both use the

T-38s to travel to their training establishments. The pilots also fly the KC-135 and specially modified Gulfstream IIs. The Gulfstreams, designated shuttle training aircraft, have been modified to simulate the aerodynamic flight characteristics of the orbiter, which glides in to land in a very steep descent path — seven times steeper than an ordinary jet airliner.

Like the real thing

Training in simulators occupies a great deal of the time of both pilots and mission-specialists. The primary machine at Houston is the shuttle mission simulator, which consists essentially of a mock-up of the shuttle orbiter flight deck mounted on hydraulic rams so that it can move realistically with six degrees of freedom — fore and aft, side to side and up and down. The instruments are connected to a computer console and appear 'live'. The simulator responds realistically in 'feel' and instrumentally to movement of the controls and operation of the switches. Three-dimensional views are projected on the 'windows' of the

cockpit mock-up which mirror those that the crew would see in real-time flight.

The mission-specialists practice payload operations with other simulators, including Johnson's manipulator development facility. This comprises a full-scale payload bay mock-up, complete with replica remote manipulator arm and aft flight-deck console, from which the arm is operated.

Training becomes more intense as crews are assigned to particular missions and the launch date approaches. Each member of a crew receives cross training in another's major duties so that they can take over the other's tasks in an emergency. In the last few weeks before the flight, the shuttle mission simulator is linked with Mission Control, and the crew go through a simulated countdown and launch. Later this is repeated on the launch pad with Kennedy launch control as well. When the astronauts finally make it into space they will have been through it all before and be able to carry out their duties with maximum efficiency.

In the weeks leading up to a shuttle mission, the crew conduct a full-scale mission simulation with Mission Control, which is also at Houston. Seen here during a simulation at the Capcom (capsule communicator) console are Mary Cleave and Bryan O'Connor. The Capcom on every mission is a practicing astronaut who has been intimately connected with the operations.

Right
This is one of the ways
shuttle astronauts can
leave the launch pad area
if danger threatens, in an
M113 armored personnel
carrier. Then of course
they would batten down
the hatches, helping to
protect them from fire and
blast.

Left
Very specific training takes place for spacewalking; always a potentially dangerous occupation. The Apollo moonwalks, for example, were rehearsed thoroughly on an imitation lunar landscape at the Kennedy Space Center. Here Apollo 15 astronaut David Scott is manning a drill that will on the Moon extract core samples of rock. Note behind him a terrestrial version of the lunar rover. Apollo 15, in July 1971, saw the first use of the rover on the Moon.

Right
Soviet cosmonauts during water egress training. They always plan to land on the ground inside the re-entry capsule of Soyuz, their now rather archaic ferry ship. But if things go wrong they must be prepared for a splashdown on water.

Rocketing into Orbit

For those who seek to escape the bonds of Earth and travel into space, gravity presents a formidable barrier. It is no small wonder that mankind took so many millennia to break from its grasp.

In our ordinary experience what goes up must come down. Birds and planes temporarily overcome gravity when they fly through the air, but they must eventually return to the ground. Gravity always wins. When you fire an Armalite rifle into the air, the bullet travels upwards initially at a speed of some 2000 mph (3000 km/h). But it soon slows down and plummets back to Earth, entrapped by gravity.

However by doing this we are getting somewhere towards breaking gravity's hold, because the more powerful the propellant in the ammunition, the faster the bullet travels from the rifle muzzle and the higher it climbs before gravity hauls it back. So gradually we are starting to beat gravity by speed. If we could fire a bullet fast enough, we should be able to overcome gravity completely and get the bullet into space so that it never comes down. A simple calculation reveals that the bullet would have to travel straight up at a speed of no less than 25,000 mph (40,000 km/h) to escape gravity. This, the Earth's escape velocity, is over 12 times the speed of an Armalite rifle bullet!

Falling free

However, there is another way we could get a bullet or any other object into space at a lesser speed. If we fire it up at an angle so that it travels eventually in a circle around the Earth, we need give it a speed of 'only' some 17,500 mph (28,000 km/h). At this speed, orbital velocity, it will continue circling the Earth in orbit. It is still within the clutches of gravity, and still dropping towards the Earth, but the rate at which it falls is equivalent to the rate the Earth's surface curves away. In effect it remains at the same distance above the surface as it moves. We refer to it as being in a state of free fall.

Even orbital velocity is incredibly high by normal terrestrial standards — over eight times the speed of the fastest supersonic planes. But it is within our reach, thanks to the invention made by the Chinese a thousand years ago, of the rocket. The Russian 'father of astronautics' Konstantin Tsiolkovsky first put forward the concept of using rockets to launch bodies into space before the

As clouds of steam and smoke billow from the launch pad area, the space shuttle blasts off from Kennedy's Complex 39. Within a quarter of an hour the orbiter will be circling silently in space, traveling at 17,500 mph (28,000 km/h).

Left
Soaring into the heavens in December 1968 is Apollo 8, crewed by Frank Borman, James Lovell and William Anders. They are bound for the Moon, though only to orbit, not to land. They blazed a trail that led others during the next four years to make six successful landings. It was the first manned flight of the gigantic Saturn V launch vehicle.

Inset: The Apollo 11 astronauts took this picture of their home planet as they sped to a lunar rendezvous in July 1969. The land masses of Africa and the Middle East are clearly visible.

Right
Russian cosmonauts still travel into orbit in expendable vehicles called Soyuz. This Soyuz craft took part in the Apollo-Soyuz Test Project in 1975.

turn of this century. He was working out the principles of traveling into space even before the Wright brothers had managed to solve the problems of powered flight in the atmosphere!

For space flight the rocket has unique advantages over the kinds of engines that power our cars, trucks and planes. It is completely self-contained, carrying not only its fuel but also the oxygen to burn its fuel. Any engine designed to work in the confines of Earth can rely on the oxygen taken in from the atmosphere to burn its fuel. Rocket engines on the other hand do not need an external source of oxygen and can function in the vacuum of space as well as in the atmosphere.

The power of reaction
Essentially, rockets work by burning their propellants — fuel and oxidizer (oxygen provider) — in a chamber to produce hot gases. The hot gases expand at high speed and escape backwards through a nozzle. The force of these gases escaping backwards gives rise to an equal force forwards which propels the rocket. This follows from Isaac Newton's famous third law of motion: 'To every action, there is an equal and opposite reaction.'

Another reason why rockets are essential for space flight is that only they can develop the power that can accelerate a craft to space-flight speeds. But to do so they must burn fuel and oxidizer at a prodigious rate. To lift itself from the launch pad, the Saturn V/Apollo Moon rocket had to burn one ton of kerosene fuel and two tons of liquid oxygen every second. Most of its 365-ft (111-meter) length and 6½-million pound (3-

The Apollo 12 command module, all that remains of a 365-ft (111-meter) stack that boosted Charles Conrad, Richard Gordon and Alan Bean to the second Moon landing in November 1969. You can see it at the Visitors Center in the Langley Research Center at Hampton, Virginia.

An aerial view of the world's premier spaceport, the Kennedy Space Center. Dominating the scene is the colossal VAB, the Vehicle Assembly Building built for assembling the Apollo moon rockets and now modified to handle the space shuttle. Beyond the VAB is the 3-mile (5-km) long runway on which the shuttle orbiters land when they return to base.

The shuttle stack, comprising orbiter, external tank and solid rocket boosters, emerges from the VAB and travels at a ponderous pace towards the launch pad, some 3½ miles (5.5 km) distant. The low building on the left of the picture is the launch control center.

million kg) weight was devoted to propellant and propellant tanks. The crew of three Apollo astronauts occupied a conical command module at the tip of the rocket measuring a little over 10-ft (3-meters) high.

Aiming for the Moon

So there were the three astronauts inside their tiny Apollo spacecraft, lifting off into space on top of millions of pounds of high-explosive fuel: kerosene, liquid hydrogen and liquid oxygen. As they accelerated, faster and faster, the first rocket stage ran out of fuel and separated. The second rocket stage then fired and propelled the remaining part of the craft still faster until it too ran out of fuel and separated. Both of these spent stages plummeted back to Earth and smashed to pieces when they impacted on the ocean. Finally the third stage boosted the Apollo spacecraft to orbital speeds and then shut down. Later the third-stage rocket fired again to thrust the spacecraft to near escape velocity and speed it on its way to the Moon. Then it too separated.

This system of constructing a launch vehicle of a number of separate stages joined together is known as the step-rocket principle. Launch vehicles have to be designed like this because no single rocket by itself has a high enough power-to-weight ratio to achieve orbital speed. A space launch vehicle must shed its rocket stages in turn so that it becomes lighter and lighter. Then the final stage with whatever payload is being carried can reach space-flight speeds.

The Apollo spacecraft, consisting of command and service modules (CSM) and lunar module, reached the Moon after about two and a half days. Two of the astronauts descended to the surface in the lunar module, explored it on foot and then returned via the ascent stage of the lunar module to the CSM. The ascent stage was discarded. Then the CSM headed for home.

Surviving re-entry

By the time the Apollo CSM reached the vicinity of the Earth, it was traveling at near escape velocity once again — 25,000 mph (40,000 km/h). Then the astronauts jettisoned the service module and swooped down into the Earth's atmosphere. They had to re-enter the atmosphere at exactly the right

angle. At too shallow an angle they would simply bounce off the atmosphere and disappear into the depths of space, doomed to journey for ever in solar orbit. At too steep an angle, they would dip too quickly into the dense region of the atmosphere, known as the troposphere, and burn up like a meteor.

Within minutes of re-entry, at the correct angle, however, the atmosphere had done its job, and slowed down the Apollo spacecraft to a speed low enough for parachutes to open, which then lowered the craft to a gentle splashdown at sea. Three hundred and sixty-five feet (111 meters) of expensive pristine hardware went up; only a tiny blackened cone a little over 10-ft (3-meters) high came back.

The Saturn V/Apollo flights were symbolic of the early phase of manned space flight, of the throwaway, disposable era. The hardware was designed to be expendable, which represented a great waste of resources.

Clearly, in the long term this was not the way to do things. It would obviously be more sensible to design a space transportation system that could be used again and again. And on 12 April 1981, such a system went into operation in the United States. That day nearly a million people at and around the Kennedy Space Center witnessed the beginning of the next stage in man's conquest of the heavens with the spectacular and highly successful first launch of the space shuttle.

While the United States forged ahead with an increasingly ambitious shuttle program, Russia still ferried cosmonauts into orbit in their relatively archaic Soyuz spacecraft, a modular expendable craft designed in the '60s. But in the early '80s they too began to develop a reusable shuttle craft.

Carried by a massive crawler transporter, the shuttle stack nears the launch pad. The orbiter is *Columbia*, getting ready to make its historic second flight in November 1981, which will mark the first time that any spacecraft has returned to orbit. Note that the external tank is painted white. This practice has now ceased, and the tank is now orange-brown, the color of the insulation sprayed on to prevent the propellants it contains (liquid oxygen and liquid hydrogen) from boiling away.

Main picture: The recovery ship *Liberty* tows a solid rocket booster back to the Kennedy Space Center after retrieving it from the Atlantic Ocean, where it splashed down a few minutes after take-off.

Inset left: Lowered by three parachutes, a solid rocket booster makes a gentle splashdown.

Within a short while it will be taken in tow by a recovery ship and returned to the launch site for refurbishing.

Inset right: The external tank, just after it has been cut loose from the orbiter. Its usefulness over, it will now plummet back to Earth, smashing to pieces as it plunges into the Indian Ocean.

Above
On a pillar of flame and smoke the shuttle soars into the heavens on its maiden flight on 12 April 1981. Shortly, the booster rockets will separate and parachute back to Earth. The orbiter's main engines will fire for another six minutes longer.

In orbit way above the Earth's cloud-flecked atmosphere, orbiter *Challenger* is pictured on its second journey into space. Inside the cavernous payload bay are the pods which held two communications satellites, launched earlier.

Once in orbit the astronauts have a heavy work load. The pilot-astronauts keep a watchful eye on the cockpit instruments, checking that all systems are A-OK. This picture shows the first shuttle commander John Young catching up on some paper work after his historic first lift-off.

An aerospace vehicle

The main component of the American space shuttle is the delta-winged orbiter. Some 122-ft (37-meters) long and with a wing-span of nearly 78 ft (24 meters), it is about the size of a medium-range airliner like the DC-9. Unlike a plane, however, it has rocket engines — three of them — in the tail, and it takes off vertically, like a rocket.

On its return to Earth, it turns into an aerodynamic plane, or rather a glider, since its descent is unpowered. It glides through the atmosphere, flying by the control surfaces such as the elevons and rudder on its wings and tail, and then landing horizontally on an ordinary runway. The orbiter does not carry the propellants for its engines. They are carried in a huge external tank on which the orbiter rides piggyback into space. Additional take-off thrust is provided by the final components of the shuttle system, two solid rocket boosters (SRBs).

On lift-off, the orbiter's main engines and the SRBs fire together, generating a combined thrust of some 6½ million pounds (3 million kg). The bulk of the take-off thrust is provided by the SRBs, which, once ignited, cannot be stopped. Two minutes after lift-off the SRBs are spent, and they separate and parachute back to splash down in

the ocean. From there they are recovered and returned to the launch site.

The orbiter meanwhile, still mounted on the external tank, continues accelerating. Eight minutes into the flight, however, the tank runs out of fuel and is jettisoned in turn. It breaks up in the lower part of the atmosphere and as it impacts the ocean. It is the only part of the shuttle system that isn't recovered. The orbiter, with main engines now cut out, briefly fires the two small rocket engines of the orbital maneuvering system (OMS) to achieve orbital velocity.

At the conclusion of the mission, the OMS engines are activated again to reduce the orbiter's speed to below orbital velocity, causing the craft to drop from orbit. Traveling at 25 times the speed of sound, the orbiter plunges into the atmosphere. A layer of thick silica tiles and other insulation protect the airframe and the crew inside from frictional temperatures of up to 2900°F (1600°C). The air drag brakes the orbiter and slows it to a speed at which its aerodynamic surfaces start to function, and it glides in to land.

The usual landing site for civilian space shuttles is a few miles from the launch site at the Kennedy Space Center on a purpose-built runway 3-miles (5-km) long. But when the weather at Cape

After a much delayed but eventually flawless maiden flight, the third operational orbiter *Discovery* is about to touchdown at the Edwards Air Force Base in California in September 1984.

Canaveral is bad there are alternative landing sites available at the Edwards Air Force Base in California, at White Sands in New Mexico, and at the Vandenberg Air Force Base in California. Vandenberg is now operational as a second shuttle launch site, being used primarily for military shuttle flights and civilian flights that need to launch payloads into polar orbits. For emergency landings overseas there are suitable runways at Rota in Spain, Honolulu in Hawaii and Okinawa in Japan.

A flying brickyard

The orbiter is built much like a conventional airplane. The airframe is constructed primarily of high-strength aluminum alloy panels, frames, stringers and honeycomb structures. The structural members are generally riveted or bolted together, but where stresses are high, structures are machined from solid metal. The strong, lightweight and heat-resistant metal titanium is also used in some high-stress areas. It is because aluminum is the main constructional material that the shuttle must have a highly efficient heat shield. Aluminum weakens when the temperature rises more than a few hundred degrees.

The major elements in the heat shield are the ceramic tiles made from silica fiber. So many brick-size tiles cover the orbiter — over 30,000 of them — that it has been called the 'flying brickyard'. But the tiles have exceptional insulating properties that prevent the heat of re-entry penetrating through, even though the outside may become red-hot. The tiles are thickest and coated black on the underside of the orbiter, which bears the brunt of the re-entry heating. The tiles on the wings and other upper surfaces are thinner and coated white.

Flexible insulating felt protects regions on the upper fuselage that experience the least heating. The highest temperatures of all, however, are experienced at the nose and the leading edges of the wings, and these are protected by a carbon refractory material.

Shuttle pros and cons

Time and time again, the orbiter can return to space. But reusability is just one of the advantages of the shuttle system. Another is the enormous cargo, or payload capacity of the orbiter. Its payload bay, which is a cavernous 60-ft long by 15-ft in diameter (18 meters by 4.5 meters), can carry several satellites and other payloads into orbit at the same time. Or it can carry fully equipped space laboratories, such as Spacelab, weighing up to nearly 30 tons.

Over conventional 'expendable' satellite launching rockets, the shuttle has the further considerable advantage of being manned. The crew can check out the satellites they launch into orbit to ensure they are working correctly before they leave them. They can recover and repair ailing satellites, as happened during spectacular missions in 1984 and 1985.

Compared with the manned launch vehicles of yesteryear, the shuttle has relatively mild acceleration, no more than that experienced in some of the latest 'roller coaster' machines in fun parks — about 3g. This enables ordinary citizens to venture into space, not just superfit, supertrained, test-pilot style astronauts.

So the shuttle is reusable, puts less strain on the human body in flight and is a versatile satellite launch and recovery vehicle. So what are its disadvantages? Setting aside technical teething troubles, experienced with launch after launch, the system still requires astronauts to ride into space shackled to hardware containing millions of pounds of high-explosive fuel. The system works fine when everything is functioning perfectly, but what if something goes wrong, not just a minor hitch, but something major?

The holocaust

The answer was provided in the most spectacular and horrifying way on 28 January 1986, on what was to have been a routine shuttle mission, 51-L, the 25th shuttle flight. Carrying a crew of seven, including the first ordinary citizen, teacher Christa McAuliffe, orbiter *Challenger* made a perfect lift-off. But just 72 seconds later it exploded, stunning the millions of TV viewers watching throughout the United States, many of them school children, geared up for the Teacher-in-Space project. In an instant, commander Dick Scobee, pilot Mike Smith, mission-specialists Judy Resnik, Ron McNair and Ellison Onizuka,

payload-specialist Greg Jarvis and teacher Christa McAuliffe were dead.

As the world mourned America's first in-flight space fatalities, NASA tried to pinpoint the possible cause of the so-public disaster. Early evidence pointed to a fault in one of the solid rocket boosters, which allowed a jet of flame to blowtorch its way into the external tank, igniting the liquid hydrogen and liquid oxygen propellants in a catastrophic explosion that blew *Challenger* to pieces. From such a holocaust there could be no escape.

Challenger was the second operational orbiter, which made its space début in April 1983. The present fleet comprises *Columbia*, which pioneered shuttle flights in April 1981; *Discovery*, which first went into space in August 1984; and *Atlantis*, which soared into orbit first in October 1985.

The Orient Express

So what is the answer? Are there any safer ways to travel into space? One answer may lie in a concept considered years ago for a fully reusable shuttle. Both the booster and the orbiter would be winged and manned, the booster returning to land on a runway after delivering the orbiter high into the atmosphere. Obviously this would be far more expensive than the present system, but undoubtedly it would be safer.

But lurking in the wings, and promising to compete with the shuttles, is an entirely new generation of aerospace vehicles that will have satellite-launching capacity as well as providing ultrafast transport across the Earth. President Reagan first drew attention to this new concept of

When the shuttle lands away from home base, for example at the Edwards Air Force Base in California, it has to be flown back by jumbo jet to the Kennedy Space Center. Here at Edwards, *Columbia* is being mated to the jumbo on its first trip back to Kennedy.

a hypersonic space plane in his State of the Union address in February 1986 when, in the wake of the *Challenger* disaster, he reaffirmed the nation's commitment to space exploration.

Able to whisk passengers from Washington to Tokyo in two hours, the hypersonic space plane has been dubbed the Orient Express. It will both take off and land on a runway. It will be able to accelerate to 25 times the speed of sound through the atmosphere, arc into space, and drop down again. It should be able to launch payloads into space for a meager $100 per pound, one-twentieth of the present shuttle cost.

British Aerospace has also put forward a similar concept called Hotol (horizontal take off and landing), which could be operational from the mid-1990s. Like the American Orient Express, Hotol would be powered by a revolutionary new type of air-breathing jet/rocket engine that would function equally well in space as in the atmosphere.

Left
Chunks of wreckage from the *Challenger* disaster are offloaded at Cape Canaveral Air Force Station on 30 January 1986, two days after the catastrophe that stunned the world.

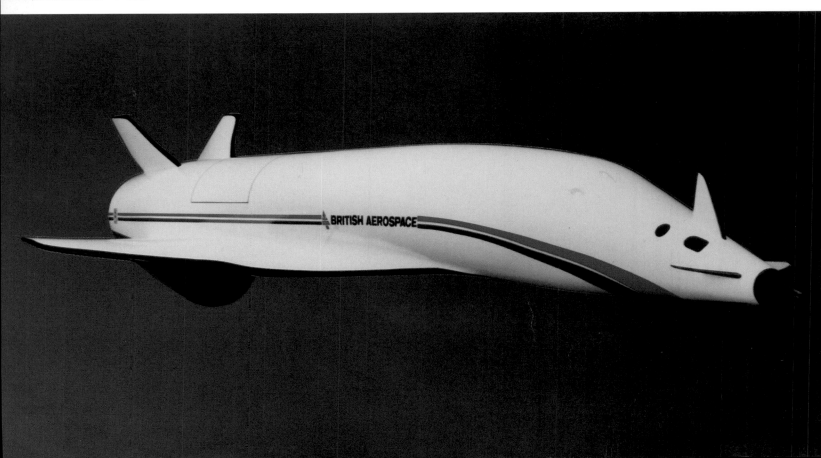

Right
The European launch
vehicle Ariane lifts off
from the launch pad at
Kourou in French Guiana.
In the wake of the
Challenger explosion,
people are wondering
whether satellite
launching should be left to
expendable rockets like
Ariane and the American
Delta rather than to
sophisticated vehicles
like the shuttles.

Left
Is this the shape of things
to come? This is a space
launch vehicle suggested
by British Aerospace,
called Hotol. Able to take
off and land like an
airplane, it will be
capable of soaring into
space and launching
satellites. The key to its
success will be a
revolutionary kind of air-
breathing engine.

Shuttle Living

Shuttle astronauts, trained to peak operational performance over the previous months, begin their journey into space approximately two hours before lift-off. It is then, with the countdown clock ticking away, that the astronauts enter the orbiter, mounted with its massive external propellant tank and twin solid rocket boosters on the mobile launch platform at Kennedy's launch complex 39.

The commander and pilot take up their positions forward, on the port and starboard of the orbiter cockpit respectively. This is located on the upper level of the pressurized crew cabin. Farther back sit one of the mission specialists and the payload specialist. Other crew members are accommodated underneath on the orbiter mid-deck.

As the countdown clock ticks down to zero, first the orbiter's three main engines fire, followed seconds later by the twin boosters. As the boosters unleash their fantastic power, the explosive bolts holding down the shuttle stack are severed, and the shuttle leaps from the pad. Acceleration forces peak at a little over 3g during the brief climb into space. By contrast, when the astronauts reach orbit, gravity apparently disappears, and they become weightless. It is not long before they get the hang of the new environment which will be their home for, typically, a week or so.

Shirt-sleeve order

Up in orbit the crew wear light clothing because their cabin is fully pressurized and air-conditioned to provide a comfortable temperature, just like an airliner is on Earth. The standard issue clothing is a striking cobalt-blue cotton coverall with full-length zip or separate jacket and trousers, and a dark blue shirt. Some crews favor shorts instead of trousers. It is a far cry from the early days of space travel when the astronauts lived in their cumbersome spacesuits.

The shirt-sleeve environment is maintained by the orbiter's environmental control and life-support system. This supplies fresh air to all parts of the crew cabin through various outlets. The composition of the air is nearly identical to that of the Earth's atmosphere, comprising 20 percent oxygen and 80 percent nitrogen. It is maintained at normal atmospheric pressure, 14.7 pounds per square inch (1 kg per square cm). The oxygen supply comes from the liquid oxygen tanks used for the on-board electrical power system, the fuel

Seven happy astronauts pose for the traditional crew portrait during the successful 51-F Spacelab 2 mission. For NASA this was an impressive milestone, being its 50th manned mission. The members of the 'Red team' of astronauts are, from left to right, Loren Acton, Roy Bridges and Karl Henize. The 'Blue team', from left to right, are John-David Bartoe, Story Musgrave and Tony England. In the striped shirt is mission commander Gordon Fullerton.

Awaiting breakfast just hours before their flight on 12 April 1985 are the 51-D mission crew. It is four years to the day that the first shuttle flight took place. Rhea Seddon is the only woman among the crew of seven. With her, from left to right, are Don Williams, Charles Walker, Karol Bobko, Jeff Hoffman, David Griggs (hidden) and Senator Jake Garn.

cells; the nitrogen from pressurized storage tanks.

To rid the cabin air of the carbon dioxide exhaled by the astronauts, the air is circulated through canisters containing lithium hydroxide. The canisters also house filters and activated charcoal to remove dust and odors from the air. The cabin temperature is controlled by circulating the air through a heat-exchanger. The excess heat from the heat-exchange system is released into space by radiators on the inside of the doors of the payload bay.

The way with water

Water is used in the heat-exchanger systems to remove heat from the cabin. It is also used for washing and drinking and mixing with food. Strange as it may seem, water is in plentiful supply on the shuttle. The reason is that it is produced as a by-product of the orbiter's electrical power system. Power is produced by three banks of fuel cells, which are so-called because they 'burn' hydrogen fuel with oxygen. The 'burning' is not by flame, of course, but ingeniously by means of a catalyst. The product of this process is water, produced at the rate of some 7 pounds (3 kg) per hour.

Running water is provided on board the shuttle for both washing and food preparation. It is supplied from the galley unit located on the port side on the mid-deck of the orbiter, which forms the living area for the astronauts. On the side of the galley is a handwashing enclosure, which is provided with both hot and cold running water. The 'running' is accomplished by means of airflow, because in the absence of gravity, of course, water won't flow from a conventional tap. Water dispensers in the front of the galley are available for food preparation.

Gourmet living

How do you fancy an evening meal starting off

Synchronizing chronographs before they climb into the orbiter entry hatch on 5 October 1984 are Kathryn Sullivan and Sally Ride, 41-G crew members. Ride will be making her second space flight. Sullivan is scheduled to make the first spacewalk by an American woman.

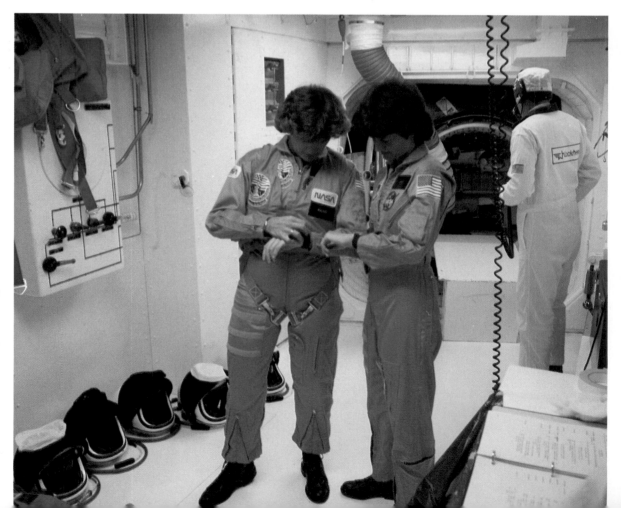

The 41-D shuttle crew favored shorts in this group portrait taken in September 1984. Judy Resnik is making her first trip into orbit. She never made it into orbit the second time, being one of the fatalities in the 1986 *Challenger* disaster. The other members of the crew are, from the left, Mike Mullane, Charles Walker, Henry Hartsfield, Michael Coats and Stephen Hawley.

with shrimp cocktail, followed by Chicken à la King and asparagus tips, with strawberries as a dessert, washed down with tropical punch? This mouth-watering selection is just one of the possible combinations that shuttle astronauts can choose from a menu that for variety exceeds that of many a downtown restaurant back on Earth. (The tropical punch is alcohol free, however, since alcohol and tobacco are banned during space flights.)

Astronauts have the standard three meals a day, and the diet is balanced so that they have a daily intake of at least 3000 calories. Each meal comes complete, packaged individually for each crew member. It comprises an assortment of packages — cans, plastic containers and plastic and foil pouches. Many of the foods are dehydrated, and require reconstituting with water from a water dispenser before eating. Some foods are thermostabilized, which means that they have been heat-sterilized and then sealed in airtight cans or pouches. Some foods have been

Pictured in a still from the IMAX/OMNIMAX film *The Dream is Alive*, the 41-D shuttle crew break for a meal. Mike Mullane (center) uses an interesting technique for eating! Behind him, Henry Hartsfield eats in a more conventional way. The other crew members in view are Stephen Hawley (right), Charles Walker (rear). Judy Resnik is almost hidden.

Below
One of the shuttle food storage drawers containing packaged food for a number of meals. Note that the packages include slices of bread, ordinary cans, and concertina-like containers — these contain beverages that require injecting with water.

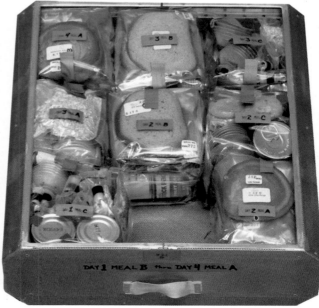

53

STS-5 astronaut William Lenoir trims pilot Robert Overmyer's sideburns in a leisurely moment on *Columbia's* first operational mission in November 1982, when it launched its first commercial satellites. Note in the background to the right an opened personal hygiene kit stuck on one of the locker doors.

preserved by irradiation, and others, including nuts and cookies, are in ready-to-eat natural form.

All members of the crew take it in turn to prepare the meals, working at the galley, which contains a pantry, oven, meal trays, wet wipes (for cleaning) and utensils. The 'chef for the day' removes the day's meal packages from a storage locker, rehydrates or heats the foods where necessary, and then assembles them on member's individual food trays. Usually it takes less than half an hour to prepare a meal.

The shuttle foods are in fact not too far removed from those served by our airlines. And they are certainly a far cry from the tasteless goo served up to the early astronauts, who ate ribbons of liquid food squeezed from toothpaste-type-tubes. Shuttle astronauts eat with ordinary spoons and forks, which perhaps seems strange in zero-g. But the stickiness and surface tension of the food keeps it on the fork or spoon as long as there are no sudden starts or stops when eating.

Wash and waste

Little washing-up needs to be done on the shuttle. The food containers are disposable, and utensils and food trays are cleaned with wet wipes. The trash is stowed in plastic bags for taking back to

Earth. It is not thrown away into space. In the confined space inside the orbiter, cleanliness is essential if the spread of disease is to be prevented. Studies have shown that in confined weightless conditions, certain microbes can multiply at an alarming rate. So the crew must keep the dining area, galley and mid-deck area generally spotlessly clean. They use germicidal cleansers, general purpose wipes and a portable vacuum cleaner. Particular attention has to be paid to the shuttle toilet, or waste-collection system, which is located to the right of the entrance hatch on the orbiter mid-deck.

The shuttle toilet, which deals, as NASA delicately puts it, with 'digestive elimination', takes the form of a commode with a separate hose for collecting urine. The hose has a cup device at the top suitable for both sexes. The toilet bears a passing resemblance to a terrestrial water closet, except that it is fitted with a seat belt and foot restraints! It also works by flushing, but the flush is provided by a stream of air rather that water as it is on Earth. The air stream is necessary to remove the body wastes, which would otherwise remain where they emerge from the body, with predictably unpleasant results.

The urine is drawn through the hose into a

waste water tank, which also holds the waste wash water. It is periodically dumped overboard, where it immediately evaporates in the vacuum of space. The solid waste is shredded by the rotating vanes of a so-called slinger and deposited on the walls of the commode chamber. Afterwards the chamber is exposed to the vacuum of space, drying the solid waste, which is returned to Earth.

Personal hygiene is also a more than desirable quality in the confined shuttle cabin, carrying a crew of as many as eight astronauts. The crew are issued with a comprehensive personal hygiene kit containing toothbrush and paste, dental floss, anti-chap lipstick, brush and comb, nail clippers, shaving cream and safety razor, skin cream, stick deodorant, seven cotton washcloths and three cotton towels. In addition the crew change their underwear every two days!

The luxury of a shower, enjoyed by Skylab crews, is not available on the shuttle through lack of space — though there would be ample water. So the astronauts must be content with a sponge bath. Those that need to, have a wet shave with shaving cream and safety razor in order to prevent the bristles floating off weightlessly and maybe fouling up sensitive equipment.

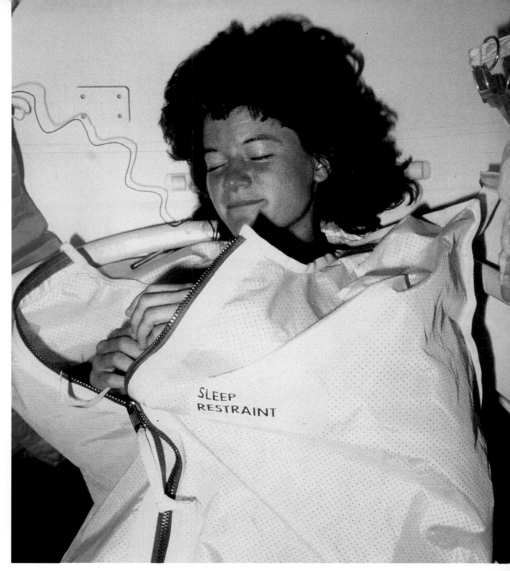

Snug in her sleep restraint is Sally Ride, during her first flight into space aboard *Challenger* in June 1983. She becomes the first American woman to venture into orbit. 'Restraint' is an appropriate term for the shuttle sleeping bag, for it does indeed restrain the astronaut from floating around the cabin.

On shuttle mission STS-8 Guion Bluford takes part in a medical experiment while exercising on the treadmill. The harness keeps his feet pressed against the treadmill.

Pilot-astronaut Robert Overmyer is pictured at the rear of *Columbia*'s flight deck. Behind him is the aft pilot's station for in-orbit activity. The window looks out into the payload bay. Notice the other window above his head.

Sleep and exercise

The shuttle astronauts also sleep on the mid-deck, on bunks or attached to the storage lockers. They sleep zipped up inside sleeping bags known as sleep restraints, which prevent them floating away. At each 'sleep-station' there is storage space for clothing and shoes. With seven astronauts sleeping at once, cheek by jowl, the optional sleeping masks and earplugs must prove a boon!

Most shuttle flights last for only about a week. And this is really too short a time for the effects of weightlessness to affect the body unduly. Exercise on board, however, is still recommended and astronauts can run on the spot on a treadmill device, wearing an elasticated harness that holds them down.

Astronauts at work

The astronauts invariably have a heavy workload for each day of their mission. Their time is split between activities on the upper flight deck, on the mid-deck and outside on EVA, in and beyond the payload bay. The commander and pilot divide their time between the front and rear of the flight deck.

The control console in the cockpit contains all the flight control and communications equipment and looks not unlike the cockpit console of a jet airliner. The main difference is that the orbiter's cockpit features three video screens, on which the astronauts can call up data on any aspect of flight operations or engineering systems from the on-board computer system.

They can alter the orbiter's attitude by means of two hand controls. A joystick, or rotational hand controller (one for the commander, one for the pilot), controls rotational movement about the

The solar maximum mission satellite (*Solar Max*), target for the 41-C shuttle mission in April 1984. *Solar Max* was the first satellite designed for retrieval by the shuttle for servicing or repair.

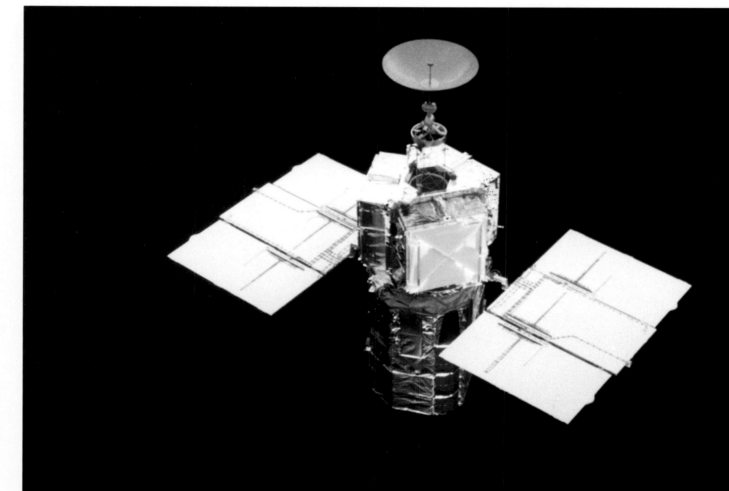

The payload bay of the orbiter is big enough to accommodate as many as three satellites, as shown here. This is the load *Discovery* carries into orbit on the 41-D mission, pictured in the payload bay on the launch pad before lift-off. All three are communications satellites that will eventually climb to geostationary orbit 22,300 miles (35,900 km) high. The two upper satellites are sprung vertically out of the payload bay. The lower one spins out frisbee style.

41-D's satellite launch frisbee style goes off without a hitch. Later a booster rocket on board will fire and thrust the satellite to high orbit above the equator.

Back at Houston Mission Control, the deployment of the satellite is monitored, like every other on-board activity. The deployed satellite is seen on the TV screen on the front wall of the Mission Control room.

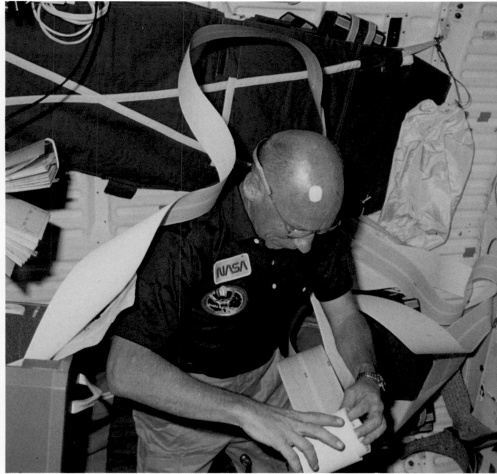

Main picture
The shuttle orbiter provides a superb vantage point for appreciating the splendors of the Earth's ever-changing landscape. Here the 41-C astronauts have photographed the verdant Nile Delta in Egypt, hemmed in on both sides by the desert sands. At the lower right is the unnaturally straight channel of the Suez Canal.

Inset picture
Senator Jake Garn submits stoically to the attentions of Rhea Seddon while participating in medical experiments abcard *Discovery* on mission 51-D. Basically an 'ordinary guy' instead of a supertrained astronaut, Garn is a prime subject for space-medicine research, and obliges the experimenters by going down with a bad attack of space sickness.

Above
On shuttle mission STS-8 Dr William Thornton used himself (note the electrode on his head) and the other crew members as guinea pigs for a series of medical experiments. Here he is checking the prolific roll of data that the space experiments have produced.

Above
Jeffrey Hoffman and Rhea
Seddon are not just
fooling around, but are
carrying out a meaningful
experiment to find the
effect weightlessness has
on this slinky toy.

Left above
No matter what the work
load, the shuttle
astronauts always find
time for a bit of fun! Here
STS-5 astronaut Joe Allen
has just thought of
something crazy to do
with his 'custard pie'!

Left below
Kathryn Sullivan (left) and
Sally Ride have created
this work of art from odd
bits and pieces they have
found floating around the
orbiter cabin. Well, at
least they're pleased
with it!

three axes. A translational controller, a lever to
the left of the commander, moves the orbiter right
or left, fore or aft, up or down. The controllers
work by firing different combinations of thruster
jets of the reaction control system (RCS). These
are located in units in the nose of the orbiter and
on either side of the engine pod in the tail.

The thruster jets of the RCS can only bring
about slight changes in orbiter velocity fore and
aft. For significant changes in velocity, as when
rendezvousing with satellites in another orbit, the
pilots must fire the two engines of the orbital
maneuvering system (OMS). The engines of the
OMS are also fired for retrobraking when the time
comes to descend from orbit.

The two hand controllers are duplicated at the
aft crew station from where many on-orbit
operations are carried out. Here the mission-
specialists work, during the times when they are
launching or checking out a satellite, or working
the remote manipulator arm, the orbiter's crane.
They can launch satellites from the payload bay in
three ways. They can spring it out of a protective
pod like a jack-in-the-box, or they can roll it out
sideways like a frisbee.

Careful manipulation
Alternatively, they can use the 50-ft (15-meter)
long flexible remote manipulator arm to literally
pluck satellites from the bay and place them in
orbit. They can see the satellites through two
windows that look into the bay, as well as get a

closer view by means of closed-circuit TV
cameras on the robot arm itself.

The mission specialists also use the robot arm
to support the most exciting part of many missions
— the extravehicular activity (EVA). Since 1984,
spacesuited astronauts flying jet-propelled
backpacks have added a new dimension to
orbital activity by repairing and recovering
satellites already in orbit. And their success has
been due in no small measure to the versatility of
the robot arm and its skillful operators.

On-board experiments can be carried out, in
rather cramped conditions, in the mid-deck area,
but for serious experimentation a special payload
is carried known as Spacelab. Spacelab is a fully
equipped space laboratory designed for
repeated use. Mission and payload-astronauts
work inside it in shifts round the clock. Off-duty
they use the crew accommodation of the orbiter.

Some of the Spacelab flights are in the so-called
pallet-mode, with instruments only being carried
in the payload bay. Control is exercised from the
aft crew station on the flight deck.

The smallest payloads carried on the orbiter
are the 'getaway specials'. These are simple
experiments that fit into standard-sized
containers, which are attached to the sides of the
bay. NASA offers room for these 'specials' to
universities, research organizations and even
schools at low cost so as to give them a chance of
sharing in the work of space exploration.

Going EVA

It is 1987 and the much delayed Hubble space telescope is at last in orbit. Seeing five times farther into the universe than any terrestrial telescope, the data it is starting to send back is phenomenal. Then suddenly one of its electronic modules breaks down, cutting off communications with Earth. For all intents and purposes, the space telescope is dead. But this project, a decade in gestation, is not finished.

On the next shuttle flight, the crew rendezvous with the 11-ton astronomical observatory and two astronauts jet over to it using self-propelled backpacks, and replace the faulty module. To these space age mechanics this is routine, part of their normal working week in orbit. Back inside the shuttle they check out the circuits and pronounce the space telescope fit and well. Within hours it is once again capturing fantastic images of distant galaxies with its 94-inch (240-cm) mirror and beaming them down to ecstatic astronomers on Earth.

Repairing Solar Max

Such a scenario would not have seemed practical even a few years ago. But today in-orbit satellite repair is, if not commonplace, a tried and tested technique. It was pioneered on shuttle mission 41-C in April 1984. On that mission a major objective was to repair a scientific satellite known as Solar Max, which had been inoperative for over three years.

The repair mission, which had been painstakingly rehearsed during training sessions in the neutral buoyancy chamber at Houston, demanded some innovative extravehicular activity (EVA) techniques. It required an astronaut to don a Buck Rogers style backpack and jet over to Solar Max, dock with it, and 'fly' it back to the shuttle, where it would be stowed in the payload bay and repaired.

Things didn't go quite according to plan, because the astronaut couldn't make a docking. But eventually the satellite was captured with the assistance of the remote manipulator arm. It was repaired, tested and relaunched. Soon it was reporting once again on the violent activity taking place on the surface of our nearest star, the Sun.

The experience with Solar Max established the basic pattern for the satellite rendezvous, recovery and repair missions that would follow — none of them planned for in the same way. The recipe for success appeared to be: two

Humor and initiative are never lacking among shuttle crews. Here on EVA, after a successful satellite recovery mission in November 1984, Dale Gardner seeks buyers for two secondhand communications satellites, which have a high mileage but have never been operated. Does he hear $30 million? Reflected in his helmet visor is fellow entrepreneur Joe Allen.

An excellent full frontal view of the shuttle spacesuit is presented in this picture of Bruce McCandless on mission 41-B. On his chest is the display and controls module, with indicators and switches that enable the astronaut to monitor and control the suit's performance.

Below
The shuttle crew has a rota for meal preparation, which usually involves adding water to dehydrated items and putting containers in the oven. Here, astronaut Gordon Fullerton is in charge. He is holding a concertina-type dispenser, while other meal packages are stuck to doors and trays by Velcro strips.

spacesuited astronauts, two jet backpacks, one remote manipulator arm and skillful operator, and a pinch of ingenious and occasionally makeshift gadgetry, together with a little luck.

Entering the airlock

In the modern space age, astronauts wear spacesuits only when they have to go on EVA. Normally they wear light clothing, thanks to the balmy 'shirt-sleeve' environment existing in today's spacecraft. But it was not always so.

For shuttle spacewalkers, preparation for EVA begins some two hours before they venture into the hostile space environment. It is then that they enter the airlock, located on the mid-deck of the orbiter. The airlock, a cylinder some 7 ft (2 meters) in diameter, has two hatches. One hatch connects with the mid-deck, the other with the orbiter payload bay. The air can be removed from the airlock without affecting the pressure in the orbiter fuselage. Two spacesuits, or EMUs (extravehicular mobility units) are kept in the airlock. For the two hours the astronauts are inside the airlock they breathe a pure oxygen

atmosphere. This is necessary to flush out nitrogen from their bloodstream. Inside their EMUs they will be breathing pure oxygen at only about a third of the atmospheric pressure. If their blood contained nitrogen, it would bubble out and give them a debilitating attack of 'the bends', a painful condition deep-sea divers experience when they decompress too rapidly.

Suiting up

Donning the shuttle spacesuit takes the astronauts surprisingly little time. And usually another crew member is on hand to help them. First the astronauts must strip off their regulation underwear and zip themselves into water-cooled 'long johns'. Then they climb into the trousers of the suit, and finally float up into the upper torso. This is easy to put on because it is rigid. Trousers and torso join in an airtight seal at the waist. Over the head goes a goldfish bowl-type helmet, and over this the EVA visor assembly.

When suiting up is complete and the astronauts are breathing air from their portable life-support system backpack, the airlock is depressurized to

Above
When moving about in the payload bay, astronauts are tethered to a safety wire along the sides, where there are also handholds. Here astronauts Donald Petersen (left) and Story Musgrave test the suits for the first time in April 1983. They work fine.

Left
Working in the payload bay of *Challenger* on mission 41-G are David Leestma (left) and Kathryn Sullivan, the first American woman to make a spacewalk. They are practicing a refueling technique for servicing satellites.

Right
For in-orbit recovery operations the remote manipulator arm proves invaluable. Here Bruce McCandless hitches a ride on the arm of the so-called 'cherry picker', which gives him a stable platform from which to work.

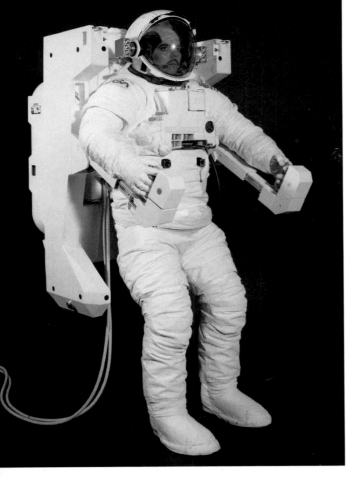

A spacesuited astronaut with a manned maneuvering unit (MMU) during ground tests. He controls the direction of flight in space by means of the hand controllers on the arms. These control the firing of different combinations of thruster jets located around the MMU.

Below
A view of the forward end of the orbiter payload bay during EVA on mission 41-B in February 1984. The two astronauts, Bruce McCandless (left) and Robert Stewart, have just emerged through the airlock hatch and have taken their positions at the two flight support stations where the MMUs are stored.

match the vacuum of space. The external hatch is opened and they can float out into the orbiter payload bay. They must take care not to exit too vigorously otherwise they could find themselves cartwheeling away from the orbiter into open space.

If they are to remain working in the payload bay, they must now snap their safety line onto wires that run along each side of the bay. This is similar to the kind of system yachtsmen use to secure themselves in heavy seas. Many in-orbit tasks, however, will require one or more of the astronauts to leave the orbiter and travel untethered to rendezvous and often dock with an orbiting satellite. This is the technique pioneered on the 41-C mission.

The manned maneuvering unit

The form of motive power the astronauts use for untethered travel, already simply referred to as a jet backpack, is correctly termed a manned maneuvering unit (MMU). Two MMUs are usually carried on board the orbiter, being stowed at flight support stations on the right and left at the front of the payload bay. The astronaut backs into the MMU, which snap-fits over his portable life-support system backpack. He can move in any direction he chooses by firing little jet thrusters dotted around the MMU — there are 24 in all. Different combinations of thrusters come into play depending on how he (or she) wants to move.

The controls for firing the thrusters are located at the end of the MMU's adjustable arms, on which the astronaut rests his own arms. The left hand turns the controller for translational movements — for motion in a straight line, back or forth, left or right, up or down. The right hand turns the controller for rotational movements — that is, rotation about the three axes.

The gas supply for the thrusters comes from twin tanks of compressed nitrogen, which are sufficient to support an EVA of about six hours. Power to work the MMU is provided by two silver-zinc batteries. They and the gas supply can be recharged at the flight support stations.

Working the 'cherry picker'

For most in-orbit activities, the remote manipulator arm, the shuttle's 'crane', is brought into play. It has proved remarkably versatile, not only doing the things it was designed for, such as launching satellites, but for dealing with mundane problems such as the accumulation of ice around a waste water vent. The arm removed the ice with a gentle tap.

During a satellite capture mission, astronauts in

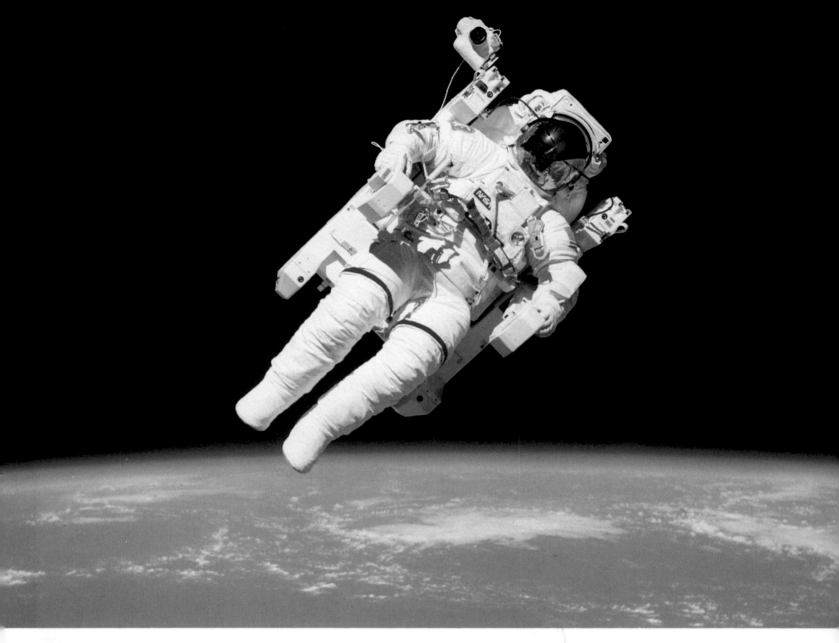

MMUs or working tethered in the payload bay operate in unison with the mission-specialist operating the manipulator arm from inside the orbiter. For EVA support, a foot restraint is often attached to the end of the manipulator arm. The astronaut uses this as a stable platform when manhandling or repairing satellites, and the arm can move him about as necessary. From its resemblance to the kind of hydraulic fruit-picking platform in common use in commercial orchards, the device has been nicknamed a 'cherry picker'.

Recovering two rogues
The mission on which the MMU was first successfully tested (41-B in February 1984) was marred by the loss of two communications satellites (comsats), Westar VI and Palapa B. The booster rockets that should have fired to lift them into 22,300-mile (36,000-km) high geostationary orbits malfunctioned, and the satellites, quite dead, drifted uselessly in low orbit.

After their success with repairing Solar Max two months afterwards, NASA decided on a

daring mission to recover the errant satellites. This was to take place in November 1984. There were problems, of course, one of which was how to physically pluck the satellites from space and stow them in the payload bay. Solar Max, however, has a built-in 'grapple' fixture which the remote manipulator arm can grip. It is designed for in-orbit servicing, as is the space telescope.

The two comsats had no such grapple fixtures, since they were destined for high orbit where the shuttle cannot venture. Then astronaut Dale Gardner, who would be participating in the mission came up with a solution — design a device with a grapple pin that fitted into and locked onto the propulsion motor nozzles of the satellites. Then the manipulator arm could grasp it. And so the device called the 'stinger' came about, officially termed an apogee kick motor capture device.

November 1984 found Dale Gardner and Joe Allen aloft in the shuttle with stingers, preparing to tackle the recovery of first Palapa B and then Westar VI. While Gardner tethered himself to the

Flying the MMU for the first time, Bruce McCandless becomes the first untethered 'human satellite', eventually jetting to a point some 300 ft (90 meters) away from orbiter *Challenger*, before returning. The MMU's performance was flawless.

The main objective of the 41-C mission in April 1984 is to repair the ailing satellite Solar Max (Solar Maximum Mission Satellite). Here George Nelson flies out to the satellite and tries to dock with it and bring it back to the orbiter's payload bay for repair. But he fails, and Solar Max is eventually captured by the remote manipulator arm.

payload bay, Allen donned an MMU and flew over to Palapa B. He inserted the stinger into the satellite's motor nozzle and locked it. He then jetted back with the satellite to the orbiter. Once there, the manipulator arm grasped it by means of the grapple fixture on the stinger.

Things started going a little wrong then, which resulted in Allen having to hold the satellite still for over an hour while Gardner installed a berthing device to it. Then they both manhandled it into the payload bay and secured it. Human muscle power and manual dexterity had saved the day. They adopted a similar procedure when they went after their second satellite. This time Gardner flew over to capture Westar VI with the

stinger. And soon that too was securely stowed. The crew returned home in triumph after scoring another spectacular space 'first'.

Flyswatting in orbit
The shuttle's satellite launching credibility was again called into question on mission 51-D in April 1985. Embarrassingly for NASA, on board *Discovery* was Senator Jake Garn, the first politician to venture into space. The trouble arose when the crew launched their second satellite, Leasat 3. This was rolled out of the payload bay, frisbee style, as scheduled. But a switch that should have activated the satellite for subsequent maneuvers didn't function.

The crew, therefore, rigged up a makeshift device that resembled and came to be called a flyswatter. During an unscheduled EVA they lashed it onto the manipulator arm and later tried to snag the switch into the 'on' position. But despite their efforts the switch refused to budge. For once human ingenuity failed. So Leasat was abandoned, but only temporarily. Even as the astronauts landed, with a bang as it happened because *Discovery* blew a tire, plans for a Leasat rescue mission were being drawn up.

And so, four months later, *Discovery* again went aloft with a crew hell-bent on restoring the 'honor of the corps' by fixing the dud Leasat. But first they successfully launched no less than three satellites to show how it should be done. Then they got down to the serious business of rendezvousing with and capturing the one that got away.

This time it was decided to forget about flyswatters and stingers and just use old-fashioned brute strength to capture the satellite manually. This was done by 'the Ox', James van Hoften, standing on the cherry picker. Then service engineer William Fisher installed new electronics in the satellite that would bypass the faulty circuits and make it amenable to command from ground station control.

Fisher did his work well, and when he had finished, Leasat's antenna unfolded. It was coming back to life. On the following day van Hoften, using sheer brute strength literally lobbed Leasat back into space. Later, on command from ground control, its boost motor fired and lifted it into geostationary orbit. $85 million worth of hardware had been saved.

It was another and most timely vindication of the shuttle system, often under attack for being

With Solar Max now safely stowed in the payload bay, George Nelson is carried by the manipulator arm to make a visual inspection. Afterwards he and fellow spacewalker James van Hoften carry out the necessary repair to Solar Max's electronics.

For satellite capture and repair in orbit, the human touch is invaluable. On the 51-A mission in November 1984 Dale Gardner is seen inserting the 'stinger' into the Westar VI satellite prior to flying back with it to the orbiter, where it will be stowed for return to Earth.

Riding the 'cherry picker' on the remote manipulator arm after the successful recovery of Palapa and Westar, Dale Gardner (left) and Joe Allen advertise the two satellites for sale. When refurbished back on Earth, they will indeed be up for sale, the first secondhand satellites ever to come onto the market.

Joe Allen struggles with the huge Palapa communications satellite prior to stowing it in the payload bay. In the right background is Dale Gardner, and in the right foreground is the 'stinger'.

too sophisticated and too expensive for ordinary satellite launches. But only the shuttle can recover and repair hardware in orbit, when things go wrong.

When disaster strikes

In such a complex activity as space flight it is inevitable that things should go wrong. The wonder is perhaps that they go wrong so infrequently. The *Challenger* disaster of 1986 reminded the world of the tightrope that the astronauts walk. One false move and there is a potential disaster, during launch, in orbit or on return to Earth.

There could well come a time when astronauts become marooned in orbit, when perhaps the retrorockets of their spacecraft malfunction, or their fuel leaks away, or they suffer a total power loss. All this could spell disaster. The Russians

seemingly had such a problem on their hands in the fall of 1983, when their space station Salyut 7 sprang a fuel leak that partly disabled it. The Soyuz ferry ship that was to join Salyut and replace an earlier rapidly deteriorating Soyuz craft was destroyed on the launch pad. The two cosmonauts on board Salyut seemed to be trapped. Would the space station last long enough until another Soyuz could be prepared for a rescue? There were suggestions that the crew might be rescued by an American shuttle. But eventually the crisis was resolved when the cosmonauts risked returning to Earth in the aged Soyuz, which fortunately remained intact during re-entry. But it could all have ended so differently.

With a fleet of three operational orbiters now, NASA is confident of coping with the problem of astronauts being marooned in orbit. There should always be an orbiter ready for launch on a rescue

There's someone knocking at the window during the 51-D mission in April 1985. Having successfully attached the 'flyswatter' to the remote manipulator arm, David Griggs grins at his colleagues through one of the windows on the aft flight deck.

Below
The 'flyswatter' on the end
of the remote manipulator
arm, after attempts to
reactivate Leasat have
failed. This part of the arm
is known as the end
effector. Inside, it has
snare wires with which it
can grip.

Right
The Leasat 3 satellite
pictured a few feet away
from *Discovery* on the
51-D mission as attempts
are made with the
'flyswatter' to snag a lever
and activate the correct
launch sequence.

mission. As there are only two spacesuits on board, the problem of crew transfer from the crippled orbiter is solved by the life-support ball, or personal rescue enclosure. This is a multilayered bag that is equipped with a portable life-support system. Astronauts from the crippled orbiter will be transferred to the rescue ship one by one inside the pressurized bag, hauled by a spacesuited astronaut.

Left
At the end of a daring satellite repair mission in September 1985, James van Hoften is pictured on the 'cherry picker' after redeploying the satellite, Leasat 3, now in full working order. The picture is taken from one of the overhead windows on the aft flight deck.

Right
The rescue ball which astronauts may use if an orbiter crew gets marooned in orbit. Correctly named a personal rescue enclosure, it measures some 34 inches (86 cm) in diameter.

Right
It's cramped inside the rescue ball, as can be seen in this plastic model, used for engineering studies. The real thing is made from triple layered synthetic fabric. It zips together and is then inflated. Inside, the astronaut has a self-contained life-support system.

Space Stations and Laboratories

In the early days of space flight in the late '50s and '60s, most of the scientific investigation in space was carried out by Earth-orbiting satellites and probes that escaped the clutches of Earth's gravity. These spacecraft monitored the space environment, looked at the Earth and into deep space and traveled to distant planets. They were essentially robots which were taking our sensors and instruments to where we ourselves could not venture.

On board the early manned spacecraft there was scarcely room for the astronauts, let alone for any scientific apparatus! Mercury astronauts could not move from their couch inside their one-man capsules. Each two-man crew of Gemini astronauts occupied a volume about the same as that on the front seat of a modern compact car. Yet one crew (Gemini 7) managed to stay in space for nearly two weeks, establishing a space duration record that stood for over five years.

The third generation American spacecraft, Apollo, was spacious by comparison with the others, as roomy as a station wagon. The astronauts could even take their spacesuits off during flight, and stand up and move around. However, even in Apollo there was no room for practicing space science. This was still the province of the unmanned spacecraft. The problems with using such an automated robot were many. Severe limitations were imposed on researchers by the need to miniaturize equipment, which had to be failure-proof if it was to be of any use.

But when the Apollo astronauts set foot on the Moon in 1969 a new era dawned. It marked a great leap forward in space science that highlighted the need for human involvement in space exploration.

No instrumented robot could describe the experience of walking on another world; or set up scientific stations to probe the environment; or carry out experiments and alter them when circumstances changed; or take instant decisions to look at something interesting that did not feature in a preprogramed itinerary.

If man is to progress at all in space exploration, then the need for a human presence cannot be understated.

The European-built space laboratory Spacelab pictured in orbit inside the space shuttle, where it stays for the whole of the flight. The version flying here features the pressurized 'long module', which connects by tunnel with the orbiter mid-deck. Twin pallets are being flown, with their instruments open to the space environment.

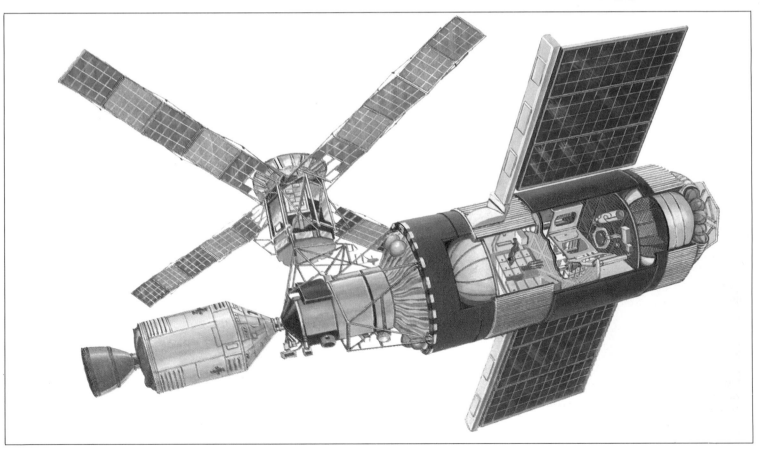

Left
This artist's impression
depicts the historic first
docking in 1971 of a
Russian Soyuz ferry craft
with the world's first
space station, Salyut 1.
Salyut 1 measures some
47-ft (14-meters) long and
is constructed of a series
of cylinders of different
diameters.

Right
How Skylab actually
looked in orbit. This
picture shows it after the
second manned crew
have left. The damaged
area is covered by sheets
of reflective material
which were effective in
preventing overheating.

Left
This artwork depicts the
American space station,
Skylab, as it should have
looked in orbit. During
launch, however, the solar
panel shown here on the
top of the orbital
workshop was ripped off,
as was the meteoroid
shield that also protected
the station from solar heat.

A fatal return

By 1970 both the United States, with the 'race to
the Moon' now won, and their Soviet rivals, were
planning projects that would keep astronauts in
Earth orbit for unprecedentedly long periods and
give them the first real opportunity to conduct
meaningful experiments in space in a variety of
scientific disciplines. The stage was set for the
launch of the world's first space stations, bringing
to reality the hopes and dreams of space-flight
enthusiasts from Tsiolkovsky onwards.

Characteristically, the Russians beat the US into
orbit when they launched their Salyut 1 space
station in April 1971. They used their standard
ferry ship Soyuz to carry crews to Salyut. The
second three-man crew to visit the space station
spent a record 24 days in orbit, smashing all
previous space duration records. But when their
re-entry capsule returned to Earth after a
seemingly perfect landing, no-one came out.
When the hatch was opened, the cosmonauts
were dead.

There was speculation that perhaps the three-
and-a-half-week stay in weightlessness had so
weakened them that they were not able to survive
the high g-forces of deceleration. But such fears
proved groundless when it was found that the
re-entry capsule had accidentally depressurized.
Nevertheless, the tragedy emphasized how
deadly the space environment was when things
went wrong. There could be no room for error.

The near abort of Skylab

The Russians attempted to place two more Salyut
craft in orbit early in the spring of 1973, but they
went out of control soon after launch. By now the
American Skylab space station was on the pad
waiting to be launched. It was a 75-ton structure
built around a rocket stage from a Saturn IB
launch vehicle.

This stage formed the main section of the
station, the orbital workshop (OWS), which
contained the main living quarters and
experimental compartments. At the front of the
OWS was the airlock module (AM), which led to
the multiple docking adapter (MDA). On the MDA
and AM, was mounted the Apollo telescope
mount (ATM). Three crews would be ferried up to
Skylab in turn over a 10-month period, each
staying for a progressively longer period. They
would travel in an Apollo command and service
module (CSM), which would dock with the MDA.
The whole cluster in orbit, with the Apollo CSM
attached, would measure over 118-ft (36-metres)
long. It would be by far the biggest structure ever
deployed in space.

Only one rocket was capable of putting such a
huge payload into orbit, a Saturn V which had
been left over from the Apollo Moon-landing
program. And on 14 May 1973 the Saturn V roared
away from the launch pad and boosted Skylab
into its intended 270-mile (435-km) orbit. Then it
became clear that something had gone horribly
wrong.

One of the two solar panels on the side of the
OWS had been torn away. The other was still
folded. Power was being generated by the solar
panels of the Apollo telescope mount, but this still
left the station desperately underpowered. Also,
the ripped-off solar panel had taken with it a

Enjoying the unaccustomed luxury of a shower is Charles Conrad, a member of the first crew to visit Skylab in May 1973. The three astronauts remained aloft for 28 days.

meteoroid shield, which also served as a sunshield to keep the station cool. As a result Skylab began to overheat. It looked as if the mission was doomed to failure before it started.

Making do and mending
The first crew should have followed Skylab into orbit after 24 hours, but instead didn't leave until 25 May. By then NASA trouble-shooters had devised a method by which the astronauts might repair the space station and make it habitable. And repair it they did, erecting a protective 'parasol' over the damaged workshop exterior. The temperature inside Skylab soon went down to a comfortable level. They also freed the jammed solar panel, allowing the generation of enough electricity to support life and work in orbit for a lengthy period.

The first Skylab mission lasted 28 days; the second, 56 days; and the third, 84 days. Record after record was smashed as the Skylab astronauts proved that human beings could live and work in weightless conditions for prolonged periods without suffering any permanent ill-effects. The second and third crews, however,

had to carry out periodic repairs to the station as their missions progressed.

By the time the final mission ended, in February 1974, Skylab was not in a very healthy state. Nevertheless NASA had hopes that it could be revitalized and pushed to a higher orbit when the space shuttle became operational. The delay in the shuttle program, however, ruled this out, and in July 1979, Skylab plunged out of orbit to a fiery destruction in the atmosphere.

A scientific bonanza
Skylab carried the largest array of scientific instruments and experimental hardware ever flown in space, and over 60 experiments were performed over a prolonged period. Among the most important were those in the field of space medicine, since Skylab provided one of the first opportunities to study the effects of long-duration weightlessness on the human body. The crew treated themselves as guinea pigs, taking regular blood samples and specimens of urine and feces for later evaluation back on earth. They monitored heart beat and circulation under exercise conditions on a bicycle ergometer. The bicycle

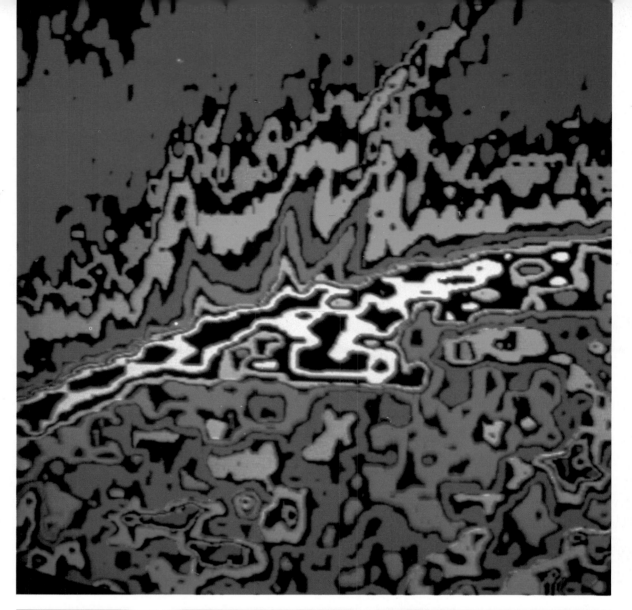

Scientifically some of the most spectacular results from Skylab were obtained from the solar studies. This false-color photograph from the solar telescopes shows a gigantic prominence, a fountain of flaming gas, erupting from the Sun's surface.

Space spider 'Arabella' still makes a pretty good job of spinning her web even in the weightless environment of Skylab. The experiment, carried out during the second manned mission, was suggested by high-school student Judith Miles.

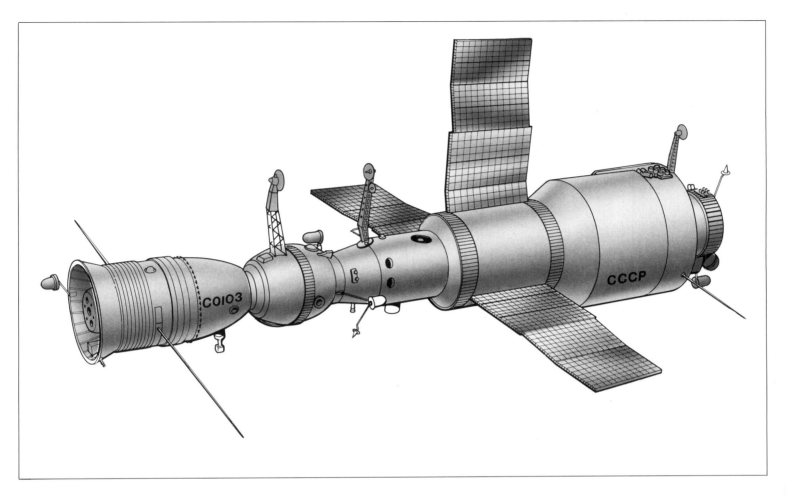

This artwork shows a Soyuz ferry docked with the space station Salyut 7. There is also a docking port at the other end, which is used by Progress supply vessels. Salyut 7 and its predecessor Salyut 6 have been the home of cosmonauts for periods of up to 237 days.

also provided them with their main means of exercise to help prevent muscle wastage.

The other major objects for Skylab study were the Sun and the Earth. The crews brought back many thousands of pictures of the Sun at different wavelengths, which revealed details unobtainable from Earth. The instruments for solar study were concentrated at the hub of the Apollo telescope mount. Thousands of pictures were also taken of Earth as part of an Earth resources experiment package (EREP). Many were produced in false color to bring out greater detail. Among technological experiments were those concerned with materials processing, such as growing crystals and brazing metals. Other Skylab experiments were suggested by American students. They ranged from incubating bacteria to studying the way spiders spun their webs in zero-g.

The Salyut record breakers

While the United States strove to get the space shuttle operational, Russia continued with its Salyut space station program. The breakthrough came with the improved Salyut 6, launched in 1977 and occupied repeatedly over a five-year period.

Salyut 6 featured two docking ports, one at each end of the station.

The reason for this design soon became apparent, when an unmanned ferry docked at one port of the station in 1978, while the crew's Soyuz craft was docked at the other. The ferry, named *Progress* and based on the Soyuz design, carried up fresh supplies, fuel and mail to Salyut. This maneuver demonstrated Russia's capability of automatically resupplying orbiting space stations and thus supporting long-stay missions.

And it was the long-stay missions of Salyut that hit the headlines. In 1978 two cosmonauts spent 139 days in orbit; in 1979 Valery Ryumin and another cosmonaut endured 175 days; in 1980 Ryumin returned to space for a further 184 days, bringing his stay time in orbit to nearly 12 months, setting an endurance record that must stand for a considerable time.

Records tumbled again when Salyut's near-identical successor, Salyut 7, became operational in 1982. One early visitor to the station was the second woman to go into space, Svetlana Savitskaya. By the year's end the duration record had been extended to 211 days. In 1983 Salyut was almost doubled in size, to about 100-ft (30-metres)

A view inside the none-too-spacious Salyut 6 in 1980 shows three Russian cosmonauts and a Cuban 'guest'. From the left, they are Valery Ryumin, Arnaldo Mendez, Yuri Romanenko and Leonid Popov. Popov and Ryumin are to stay aloft for 184 days.

Other visitors to Salyut 6 during Popov's and Ryumin's marathon stay in orbit are Russian cosmonaut Viktor Gorbatko and Vietnamese 'guest' cosmonaut Pham Tuan, seen here during training in a Soyuz capsule.

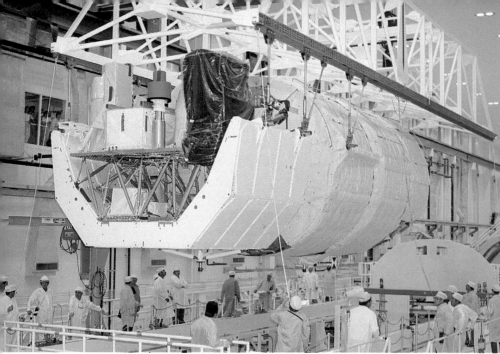

The whole Spacelab complex of pressurized laboratory and pallet is pictured before launch in the Operations and Checkout Building at the Kennedy Space Center. Later it will be installed in the payload bay of orbiter *Columbia* for lift-off in November 1983.

The emblem of the Spacelab 1/STS-9 mission, which marks a great expansion of space science. It is a joint venture of NASA and ESA, the European Space Agency. The flags are those of the nations participating in the project.

A scene on board Spacelab 1 during a highly successful 10-day mission, which began on 28 November 1983. Here four of the six-man crew check the results of one of the 70-plus experiments on a TV monitor. The laboratory is equipped with a comprehensive range of instruments and equipment and also computing facilities for early analysis of experimental data.

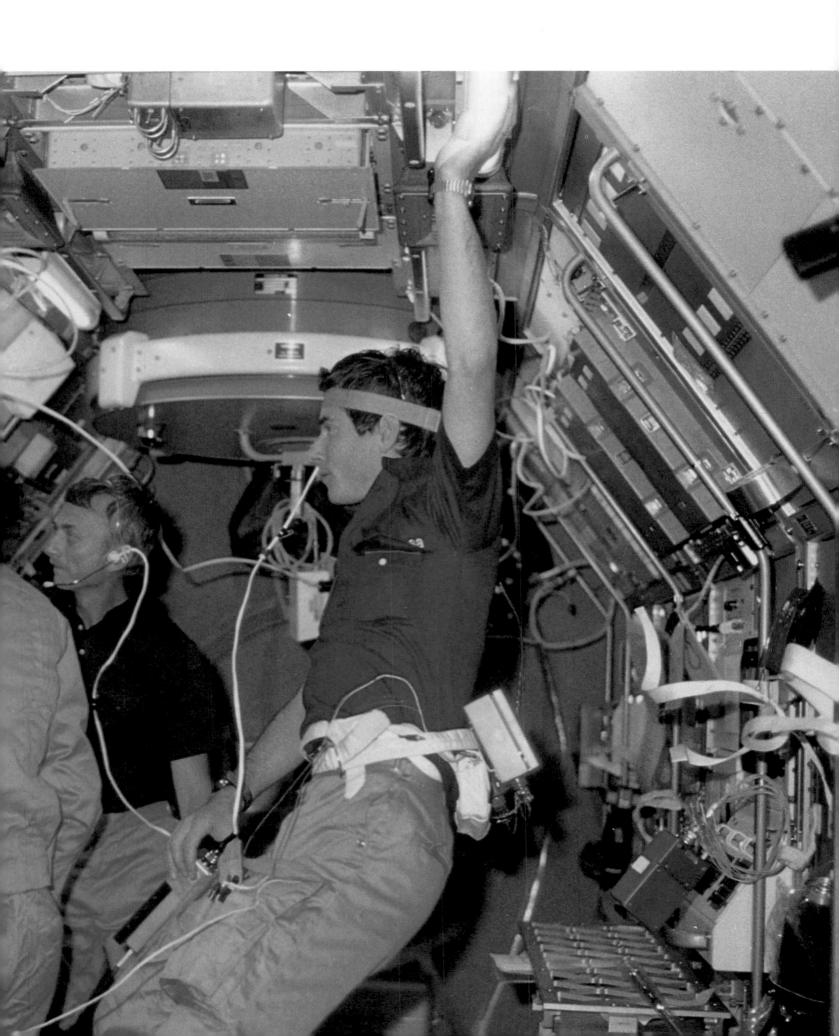

long, by the addition of Cosmos 1443, a cylindrical craft that brought supplies and provided extra working space. In 1984 Savitskaya paid a return visit to the station, where she carried out a three-hour EVA. In so doing she upstaged the two female members of the crew on shuttle mission 41-G (October 1984), beating Sally Ride to be the first woman to go into space twice and Kathryn Sullivan to be the first woman to go spacewalking.

Russia's final triumph in 1984 came when cosmonauts Oleg Atkov, Leonid Kizim and Vladimir Solovyov returned to Earth on 2 October after no fewer than 237 days in space. By then Russian cosmonauts had logged nearly 88,000 hours in orbit, more than twice that of the Americans.

Since that time, however, Salyut 7 has been in trouble. Contact with it was lost for a time in 1985, but a Soyuz crew managed to reactivate the station and its faulty systems in mid-summer. Then in late November Salyut 7's crew made an unexpected return to Earth because one of the cosmonauts was ill. It was the first time in space history that this had happened. It was yet another blow to Soviet plans to keep a permanent presence in space.

However, the Russians were by now putting the finishing touches to Salyut's successor, called *Mir* (*Peace*). And on 20 February 1986, they launched it into orbit. *Mir* is not too different from Salyut 7 in general appearance and size, but is

outfitted differently. Notably it has no fewer than six docking ports to allow simultaneous linkup with a variety of other spacecraft or purpose-built modules to be used as workshops or laboratories. Each module will have its own life-support and power system. Mir itself has twin solar panels to produce power, which are twice as large as those on Salyut 7.

Because *Mir* does not house bulky experimental equipment like Salyut, there is much more room inside for living space. There are separate small cabins for each crew member, equipped with a chair, desk and sleeping bag. The first cosmonauts to visit *Mir*, on 15 March 1986, were two of the team who participated in the marathon 237-day occupation of Salyut 7 in 1984. They were Leonid Kizim and Vladimir Solovyov.

Reusable Spacelab
Until the coming of the NASA space station in the mid-1990s, the rest of the world cannot hope to compete in flight duration with the Soviet Union. But they can and do surpass it in space science achievements. The opportunities for space science have expanded immeasurably since the introduction of the space shuttle and in particular since Spacelab became operational in November 1983 on shuttle mission STS-9.

Spacelab is a fully equipped state-of-the-art scientific laboratory built by the European Space Agency (ESA). It is designed to fit into the shuttle

The advantage of having a human presence in space is demonstrated on the Spacelab 3 flight in April 1985. When something goes wrong with one of the experiments, the astronauts open their tool kit and get to work. Tackling the problem are William Thornton (center) and, partly hidden inside the apparatus, Taylor Wang. Giving helpful advice in the background is Don Lind. The troubleshooting paid off, and Dr Wang later resumed his studies.

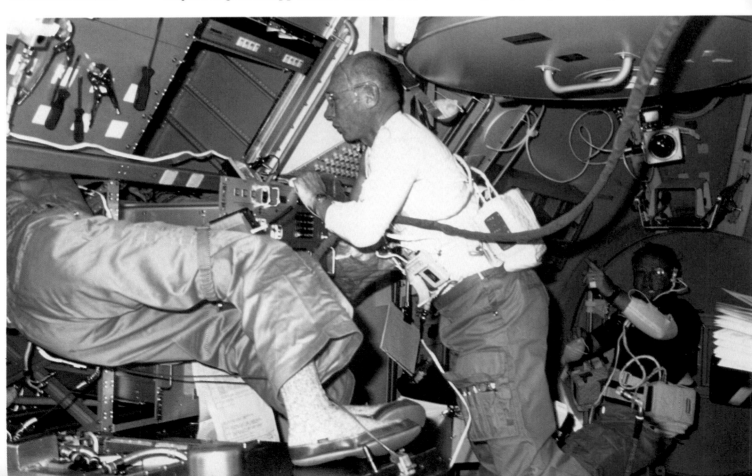

orbiter's huge payload bay and, like the shuttle, it is reusable. It can be transported into space in various configurations. A standard one is the long module. This takes the form of a twin-segment cylinder about 23-ft (7-meters) long and 13-ft (4-meters) in diameter. This module forms a pressurized laboratory in which astronaut-scientists perform their experiments and observations. It is linked by an access tunnel to the orbiter mid-deck, through a hatch normally leading to the airlock module.

Usually the long module is accompanied into orbit by one or more U-shaped pallets, on which instruments are mounted that must be exposed to the space environment. Some Spacelab flights indeed feature only the pallets.

The nine-day maiden flight of Spacelab, carried aloft by *Columbia*, was a spectacular success. Over 70 experiments were carried out round the clock by two shifts of mission and payload specialists, including West Germany's Ulf Merbold, the first non-American to fly on a US spacecraft. The experiments covered the life sciences, materials processing, space and Earth physics as well as observations.

The second Spacelab flight, actually

Right
Two squirrel monkeys accompany the human astronauts on Spacelab 3. In this picture one of them is obviously wondering why William Thornton is standing on his head!

Below
A bonus for the Spacelab 3 crew was to witness a magnificent display of the aurora; shimmering curtains of colored light caused by the impact of charged particles on the molecules in the Earth's upper atmosphere.

designated Spacelab 3, in *Challenger* on mission 51-B (April 1985), also featured the long module. It carried not only a 7-man astronaut crew but also 24 rats and 2 squirrel monkeys. Investigations ranged from observing the animals for clues to space sickness to photography of auroras and growing crystals. On mission 51-F (July 1985) flew Spacelab 2, consisting of three pallets which carried sophisticated astronomical and scientific instruments. A German Spacelab mission, Spacelab D1, on shuttle flight 61-A (October 1985), again featured the long module and carried the ingenious space sled, an acceleration device to produce g-forces artificially. It formed part of experiments on the human vestibular (balance) system which could lead to greater understanding about the mechanisms of space.

Left
The Spacelab D1 mission (61-A) that lifted off in October 1985 is dedicated to West Germany. On it the astronauts use the space sled for the first time, wearing a device for recording eye movements. Astronaut Robert Parker practices with this apparatus before the flight.

Above
Baring their arms for blood-letting are West Germany's Reinhard Furrer and Wubbo J. Ockels (mostly out of the picture) from the Netherlands. Both are payload specialists on the Spacelab D1 mission. Blood samples are taken regularly on Spacelab flights and returned to Earth for analysis, helping researchers assess the effect of zero-g on the human body.

Left
Working in the foreground inside Spacelab during the D1 mission is American mission specialist Bonnie Dunbar. At the rear is West German payload specialist Reinhard Furrer. Spacelab experiments are manned around the clock by two shifts of astronauts.

Space Station 2000

By the turn of this century 'living in space' will be taking on a new meaning for many astronauts. They will not, as now, simply be space commuters shuttling back and forth between Earth and orbit just for a few days. They will take up residence in space for periods of months at a time. For by then the NASA space station will be a reality, leading to a rapid expansion in the utilization of space.

Built up of interlocking modules and with a solar power supply, the space station will orbit about 250 miles (400 km) high. A crew of from six to eight astronauts will man the station day by day, week by week and year by year. It will be constructed *in situ* from units ferried up into orbit by shuttles. For the basic station structure at least five shuttle flights will be needed. The shuttle will subsequently visit the station every few weeks, ferrying up fresh supplies and replacement crews.

Astronomers, physicists, doctors, engineers and biologists will feature prominently among the crews, for the space station will be first and foremost a space laboratory, taking advantage of the unique vacuum and zero-g, or microgravity environment. Also aboard will be satellite service technicians and, later, construction workers engaged on even more ambitious space engineering projects.

Within the decade
President Ronald Reagan set the space station program going in his State of the Union message to Congress on 5 January 1984. "We can follow our dreams to distant stars, living and working in space for peaceful economic and scientific gain," he said. "Tonight I am directing NASA to develop a permanently manned space station and to do it within a decade."

This had more than an echo of President John Kennedy's impassioned plea in 1961 that the United States should land a man on the Moon before the end of the '60s. But the cost of the space station, estimated at some $8 billion, will be only about a third of that of the Apollo program.

In keeping with NASA's traditional policy of international cooperation in space activities, the President invited other nations to join in the space station program. By early 1986 NASA had signed memoranda of understanding with Canada (which built the shuttle orbiter remote manipulator arms); the European Space Agency, ESA (which built the Spacelabs); and Japan. All three partners then

Circling in orbit some 250 miles (400 km) above the Earth is an international space station, assembled from modules lifted into orbit by the space shuttle. It provides space and the opportunity for many kinds of scientific endeavors, from the production of life-saving vaccines to the industrial processing of high-tech alloys and electronic materials.

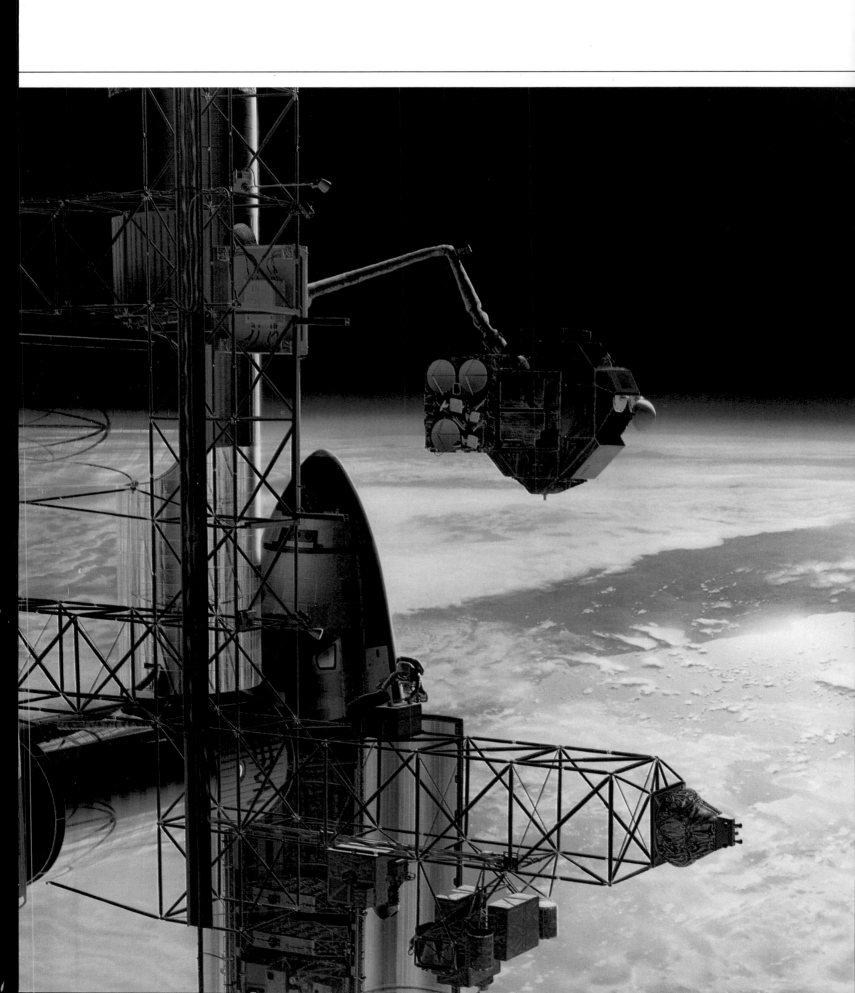

began to become involved in design studies.

Responsibility for space station design and operation falls to four main NASA centers. The lead center is the Johnson Space Center at Houston, Texas, which is also responsible for the overall structure and interfaces between the various elements. The Marshall Space Flight Center at Huntsville, Alabama, oversees the design of the main modules. The Goddard Space Flight Center at Greenbelt, Maryland, is concerned with unmanned free-flying platforms, instruments and payloads. The specialty of the Lewis Research Center at Cleveland, Ohio, is the power-generating system for the station.

Microgravity — friend and foe
Assembling a space station from parts ferried up into orbit, of course, is easier said than done. The microgravity environment poses unusual problems for construction work. Structures appear weightless but still have inertia, which is a function of their mass, not their weight. So if two massive structures collide in orbit, they can be severely damaged.

Left above
In the water immersion facility at the Marshall Space Flight Center in Huntsville, Alabama, spacesuited students from the Massachusetts Institute of Technology assemble a large space structure from interconnecting beams. They test procedures that will later be used in shuttle experiments.

Right
On the 61-B mission in November 1985, Jerry Ross works on the ACCESS construction, finding the task much easier than anticipated. The 'cherry picker' on the end of the remote manipulator arm provides him with a stable platform.

Left
It is 'Woody' Spring's turn to build, during a 61-B EVA. He adds another beam to the EASE structure, anchored in the payload bay of orbiter *Atlantis*.

This is one of many configurations that NASA has proposed for an orbiting space station. It is a concept called the Space Operations Center, and would be built up over a period of a decade or so. As in all NASA concepts, the shuttle plays a vital role.

For 'structures' also read 'astronauts'. For if a floating module or beam hits astronauts at any speed, they could be badly injured, or their spacesuits could rupture, causing instant death. So assembly techniques must be worked out which a bulkily spacesuited weightless astronaut can perform efficiently and safely.

The Marshall Spaceflight Center and the Langley Research Center in Hampton, Virginia, have been working on the problem since the mid-1970s, in conjunction with researchers at MIT, the Massachusetts Institute of Technology, in Cambridge, Massachusetts. They have practiced assembling large space structures on the ground and also in simulated weightless conditions in Marshall's large water tank, the neutral buoyancy chamber.

EASE does it

From Marshall's work evolved methods of working that could be used when space station construction begins. They appeared to be effective in simulations, but would they in real

life? To answer the question, NASA planned for structural assembly work to be a major objective on shuttle mission 61-B in November 1985.

Two kinds of assembly methods were tested, one known as EASE (experimental assembly of structures in extravehicular activity), the other ACCESS (assembly concept for construction of erectable space structures). The two

Right
This more modest station features two habitation modules (the cylinders). One of these would serve as living quarters, the other as a laboratory/observatory. Docked to the right-hand cylinder at top is a logistics module, a unit in which fresh supplies are carried from Earth by the shuttle. Underneath is an enclosed space hanger for an orbital maneuvering vehicle.

Inset picture
The habitation module would provide comfortable living conditions for a permanent crew of from six to eight astronauts. Each module would be self-contained so that if it were damaged, the rest of the station would not be affected.

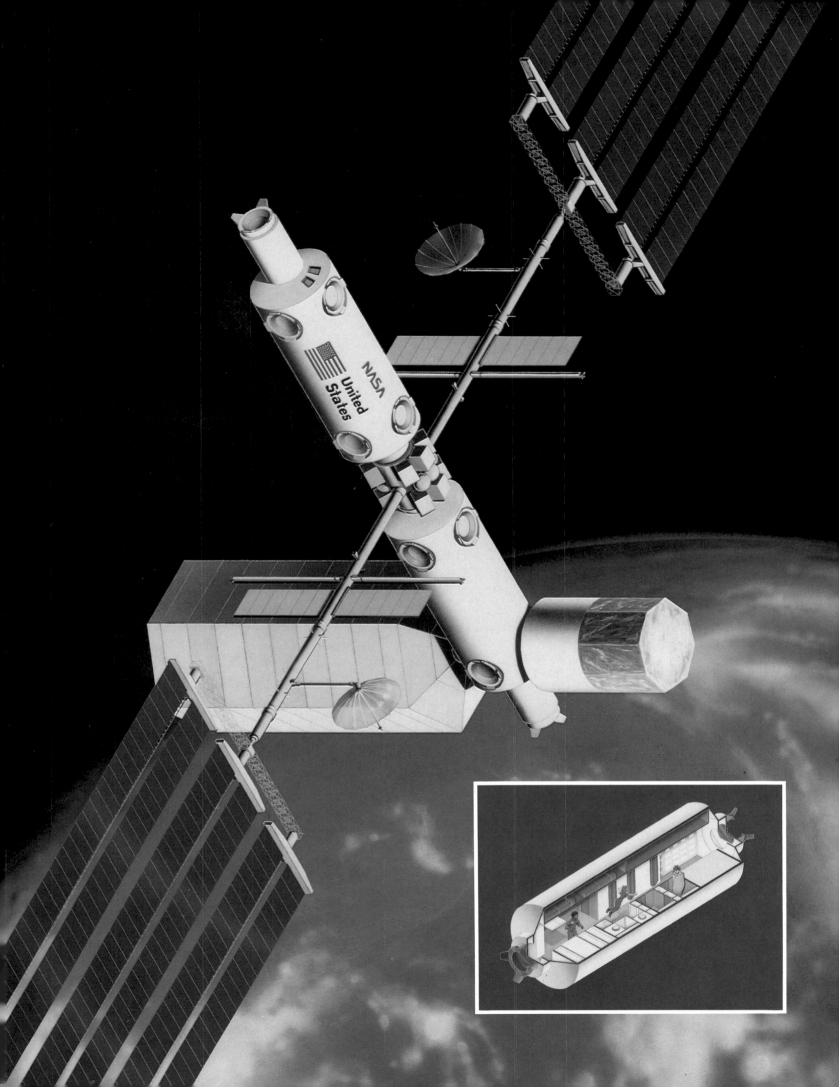

By the early 21st century a space station of this complexity could be in orbit. It will have started life as quite a simple structure and then been added to as time went by. The box-like units attached to various parts of the station, house experimental and observational equipment. Note the free-flying platform nearby.

spacewalkers assigned for the mission were Jerry Ross and Sherwood 'Woody' Spring. Assisting them from inside the shuttle orbiter (*Atlantis*) was Mary Cleave, who operated the remote manipulator arm.

During a total of over 11½ hours of spectacular EVA, Ross and Spring proved the effectiveness of the two systems, working faster than they had in underwater simulations. Using a set of guide rails they constructed a 45-ft (13.4-meter) high ACCESS tower of triangular truss design, using beams and struts that snap-fitted together in so-called nodal joints. The EASE structure took the form of a kind of pyramid made from 12-ft (3.5-meter) long beams that also snap-fitted together for ease of construction.

The astronauts dismantled then re-erected both structures a number of times, and also manhandled the finished ACCESS tower as astronauts would have to when building the real station. All the while their actions were being closely recorded on video and film and by stopwatch. Their medical condition was also monitored to rate their working ability for the various tasks carried out. After each of their two EVAs, of over five-and-a-half hours and six hours respectively, both confessed they were tired, and working with relatively inflexible EVA gloves left their hands feeling stiff and numb.

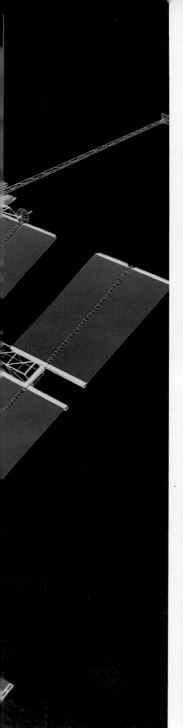

Above
This free-flying platform specializes in communications. It is located not in low orbit next to the space station but in geostationary orbit 22,300 miles (35,900 km) above the equator.

Left
Here at the Marshall Space Flight Center in Huntsville, Alabama, is a prototype beam builder, an ingenious machine that automatically manufactures lengths of trussed aluminum beams, which it fabricates from rolls of aluminum strip.

The beam builder

Ross and Spring demonstrated one method of constructing beam structures in space, but for building large beam structures, machines will eventually be used. One type of machine has already been built and tested, but not yet in space. The machine, also developed at the Marshall Space Flight Center, is called the beam builder.

It is an ingenious piece of equipment, which makes a trussed structure of triangular section continuously from three spools of aluminum strip. Three ribbons of flat strip go in one end, and a fully fabricated beam comes out of the other. The machine bends, cuts and spot-welds the aluminum in a continuous process. It could be accommodated in the payload bay of the shuttle orbiter, together with enough strip to make structures hundreds of feet long.

The modular approach

At the time of writing, a definitive design for the space station had not yet been finalized. But it appears that it will have a skeletal structure consisting of two parallel 300-ft (90-meter) long vertical 'keels', crossed by a horizontal beam supporting the solar-cell arrays that will supply the station with electrical power. The pressurized modules that form the inhabited areas will be located at the station's center of gravity.

The modules will take the form of cylinders some 44-ft (13-meters) long and about 13-ft

Using the beam builder or machines derived from it, astronaut engineers will start to tackle ambitious construction projects like this solar power complex. Note the scale of the complex from the size of the shuttle orbiter.

(4-meters) in diameter. With these dimensions they fit into the shuttle orbiter's payload bay. Any station elements larger than this will have to be taken into orbit in sections and assembled there.

The pressurized modules for the station will be of standard design but will be outfitted in different ways — as living quarters for the crew, laboratories and workshops and for housing stores and equipment. The design of the modules and their fittings will reflect the experience gained from the construction and operation of Spacelab, the modular space laboratory built by the European Space Agency.

An unsymmetrical cluster
The final space station will form an unsymmetrical cluster of modules and beams and will be dominated by the vast solar-cell arrays covering

an area half the size of a football field. Other features will include a smaller set of panels that act as radiators to rid the station of excess heat. There will also be numerous antennas for communications and attached pallets containing scientific instruments open to the space environment.

One or more cranes will be located at appropriate points on the structure to help with the unloading of the shuttle supply craft and in-orbit construction work. Probably they will be advanced versions of the remote manipulator arm now used with great success on the shuttle orbiters.

Another feature of the station will be unmanned free-flying platforms located at some distance from the main structure. Some will be mounted with a variety of instruments for Earth observation, astronomy, physics and so on. Other platforms would support space industries such as the production of ultrapure crystals for electronics and superstrong alloys for construction. In time advanced platforms would be built with modules that could be pressurized for occasional manning.

Space tugs

A major role for the mature space station will be as a permanent base for tending, servicing and repairing not only the free-flying platforms but also other satellites. A few satellites have already been repaired and recovered in orbit with spectacular success, by shuttle astronauts, but with the coming of the space station, the activity will be expanded to cover many more satellites, which would be designed specifically with in-orbit maintenance in mind.

To give them access to orbiting satellites, the space station service engineers will enlist the support of a little space tug called an orbital maneuvering vehicle (OMV). Such a machine is already under development and should be flying by the early 1990s. It will probably be used in the construction of the space station itself.

Essentially the OMV is a reusable rocket propulsion unit equipped with a docking mechanism so that it can link up with platforms or satellites, and boost them back to the vicinity of the space station, where they can be serviced or repaired. It will then return them to where they came from. The OMV will also be used to launch satellites into orbits hundreds of miles higher than the shuttle.

Many satellites, particularly communications satellites, need to operate in geostationary orbit some 22,300 miles (36,000 km) above the Earth. The OMV will not be powerful enough to boost them to this height, so a second type of space tug will be built, called an orbital transfer vehicle (OTV). This again will be a reusable rocket stage with a built-in docking mechanism and will also be capable of retrieving satellites from high orbits.

Satellite power

The space station will be an on-going project because over a period of years it will be expanded by the addition of extra modules and other facilities. It could take over other roles in the future, such as a spaceport for lunar excursion vehicles and interplanetary craft. It could also serve as a base for the construction of more exotic space structures, such as mammoth communications complexes and power satellites.

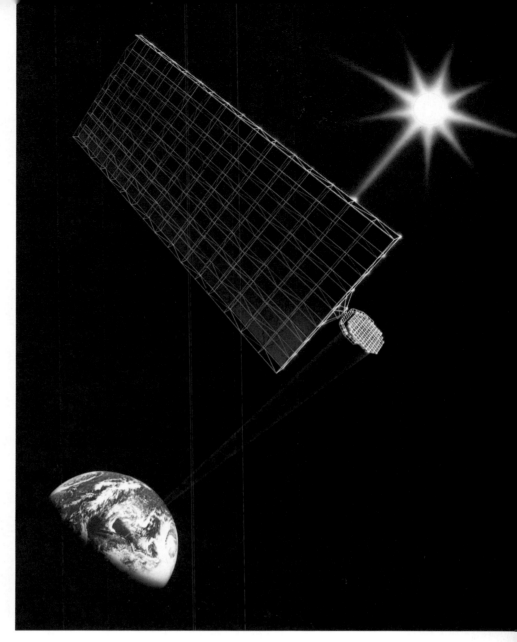

Solar power satellites (SPSs) are an attractive proposition in theory. They would harness the abundant energy that is continually flowing towards the Earth from the Sun. The satellites might take the form of giant arrays of solar cells of the type already used to power spacecraft, or they might consist of huge reflectors that would concentrate solar energy onto boilers that would drive turbogenerators. The power they generate would be converted into microwaves and beamed down to Earth, to be collected there by large antennas.

In practice SPSs present massive problems, 'massive' being the operative word. For to produce an electricity output on Earth of a large conventional power station, the SPS would need to have dimensions measured in miles. A typical solar-cell SPS could be some 7-miles (12-km) long and 2.5-miles (4-km) across and weigh some 20,000 tons. A workforce of some 500 people would be required to build it! Though attractive in theory, therefore, SPSs do not look like a good bet for solving next century's global energy problem.

This picture shows the concept of a solar cell power-satellite. The cells would convert solar energy into electricity which would in turn be converted into microwaves and beamed down to Earth. The satellite would be in geostationary orbit so that it appeared fixed over a particular spot.

When large-scale space
construction work really
gets under way, new
heavy-lift launch vehicles
will be needed to carry
the many tons of materials
into orbit, a job beyond
the capability of the
shuttle fleet. Boeing
Aerospace have
proposed this idea for a
heavy launch vehicle,
which would be reusable.

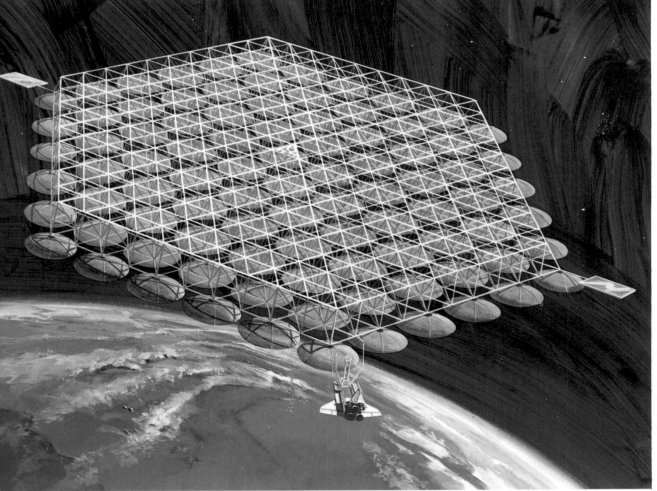

Communications has
perhaps undergone the
greatest revolution since
the beginning of the
Space Age. And in the
next century
geostationary orbiting
communications
complexes like this will
be built. They will be
powerful enough to
transmit signals between
personal communications
devices, such as wrist
radios.

Right
Astronauts by themselves
will be unable to tackle
large-scale construction
work and will have to
enlist the help of robot
and human-controlled
machines, maybe like the
ones shown in the picture.
Other machines would be
free-flying robots
controlled remotely from
a construction control
center.

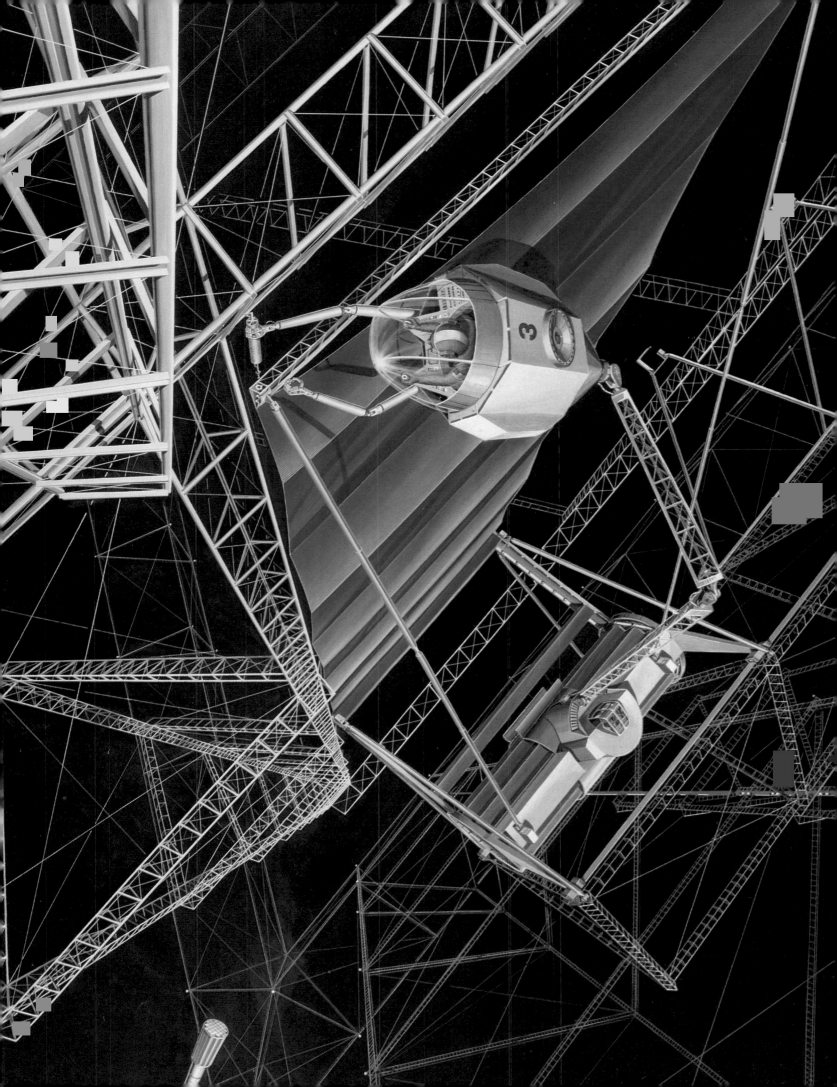

Colonizing the Solar System

The space stations of the 1990s and the more elaborate structures they will help create in the next century will serve as the springboard for the expansion of Man's influence way beyond the confines of his home planet. Inevitably the first target for human colonization will be the only other world we have visited besides our own — the Moon. We know we can get there, and we know what conditions there are like.

A permanent base on the Moon, in turn, could provide the necessary facilities for the construction of gigantic colonies in space some quarter of a million miles (350,000 km) away, in which thousands of people might eventually live for their whole lives. By then manned exploration of our relatively close planetary neighbor Mars would be well underway. By then also we might well have made contact with extraterrestrial civilizations, and taken tentative steps along the path that will ultimately take us to other planetary systems around other stars.

Lunar Base One

The establishment of a permanent lunar base could come within a few decades. To start with it would be a very makeshift structure, composed perhaps of converted empty rocket fuel tanks, covered with lunar soil for protection against meteorites. The first people to inhabit the base would be scientists, engineers and miners. While the scientists proceeded with the wider exploration of the Moon's surface, capitalizing on the Apollo experience, the miners and engineers would set up operations to mine and process lunar minerals into metals, glass and concrete. With materials such as these the permanent base would be built.

Analysis of the lunar soil and rocks brought back by the Apollo astronauts has revealed the presence of sufficient quantities of aluminum, iron and titanium ores that would be suitable for smelting into structural metals. The permanent base could well be much like an Earth-orbiting space station but located on and under the surface. It would be built of pressurized modules, isolated from one another for safety. Eventually there would be larger domed areas to relieve the otherwise claustrophobic conditions and even

One of the most breathtaking concepts advanced for future space exploration is that of the space colony, floating hundreds of thousands of miles away in a stable location in the Earth-Moon gravitational system. The colony depicted here comprises a pair of so-called O'Neill cylinders, inside which there would be a simulated Earth landscape where agriculture would be a major activity to support a population of thousands.

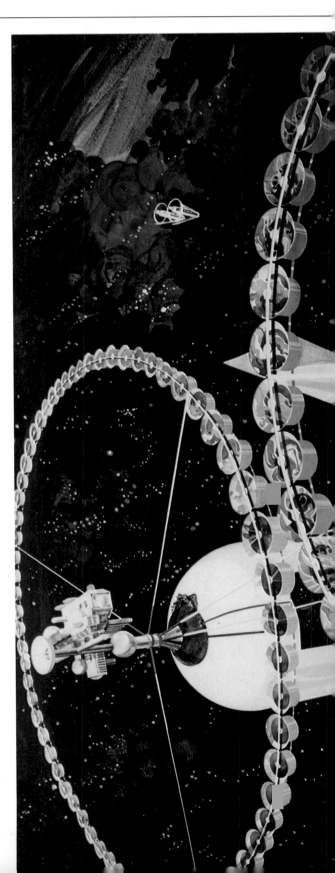

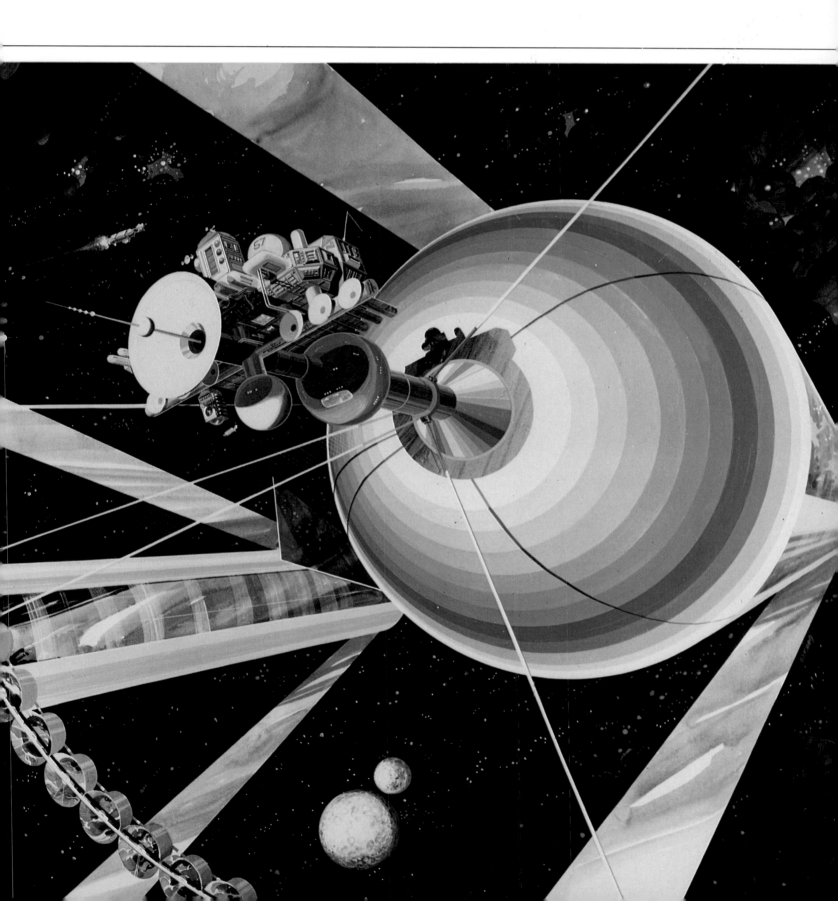

Left
Come next century the
Moon will once again
command our attention
and will be used as a base
for exploration and
observation. Here a lunar
ferry is about to depart
from the vicinity of an
Earth-orbiting space
station, destination, the
Moon.

Above
In the most exciting
adventure of all time, 12
Apollo astronauts
explored the Moon in the
late '60s and early '70s.
Here Apollo 16 astronaut
Charles Duke drills down
to extract a core sample of
rock whose layers will
reveal much about the
history of the Moon. The
Apollo missions told us
much about the Moon but
also whetted our appetite
for further knowledge.

Right
One way lunar
exploration may proceed
is via an orbiting lunar
station not dissimilar to
that envisaged for Earth
orbit. From the lunar
station, exploring
astronauts would make
regular sorties down to
the surface, where they
would establish base
camps to support their
expeditions.

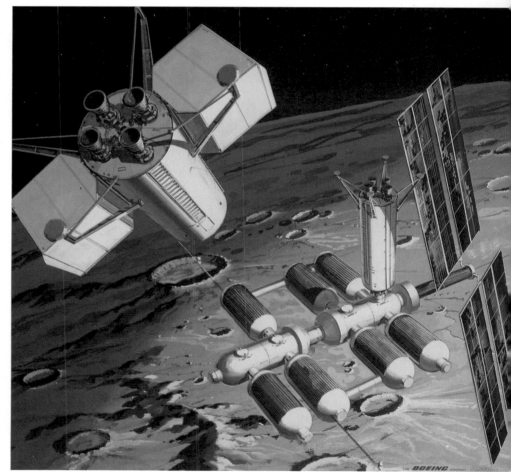

provide space to grow crops for feeding Moon-base personnel.

Providing life-support

The atmosphere inside the Moon base, of course, would have to be artificial, since the Moon is too small a body to retain any atmosphere of its own. Strangely enough, there would be no problem about the provision of life-giving oxygen on the Moon. Lunar rocks contain an abundance of oxygen-bearing minerals which could readily be processed to yield the precious gas.

The other major life-support necessity, water, does, however, present more of a problem. As everybody knows, water is a chemical combination of hydrogen and oxygen. On the Moon hydrogen is lacking and so it would have to be ferried to the Moon base from Earth in the form of liquid hydrogen. Careful recycling of this chemically produced water would ensure that minimal hydrogen was consumed.

The provision of power would also be a problem. Solar power would provide only half the answer, because for two weeks out of four any part of the lunar surface is in darkness. Fuel cells might provide a temporary solution for the first small band of explorers, but it would require a steady supply of precious hydrogen. In the long term a nuclear power plant would fit the bill. There is plenty of radioactive material on the Moon, some concentrated curiously in 'hot spots' located by Apollo spacecraft from lunar orbit.

Magnetic catapults

As the Moon orbits around the Earth every month, it always presents the same face towards us. Astronomers say it has a captured rotation. And the main lunar bases will be built on this near side, ensuring continuous communications with Earth. Astronomers, however, will eventually build another base on the Moon's far, hidden side.

The reason for this is that optical astronomers will be able to view the heavens free from the 'glare' of earthlight (some 50 times stronger than moonlight), and radio astronomers will be able to 'listen' to the heavens free from radio interference from their home planet.

As time goes by, the lunar base would start exporting the ores it mines. These would form the raw materials for the construction of space colonies — huge cities that would float in deep space and be the homes of thousands. Because of the low lunar gravity (only one-sixth of the Earth's), it would be far easier to ferry materials from the Moon than from the Earth. And in any case, on Earth we will increasingly need to hang on to all the materials we have.

The constructional materials destined for the space colonies would be processed, not on the Moon, but near the construction site in space. They would be transported into space in an ingenious way, by a kind of electromagnetic catapult known as a mass driver. The mass driver would consist of a series of buckets holding bags of ore which would be accelerated along a track by magnetic forces to a speed of some 1.5 miles (2.5 km) a second. This speed, lunar escape velocity, is the speed a body needs to escape from the Moon's gravity. When the buckets achieved this speed, they would be slowed down, but because of inertia, the bags of ore would shoot out of them into space.

In space the bags of ore would be collected in a huge net and towed by a space tug to the colony construction site. This would be located at a point in the Moon's orbital path around the Earth that is some 240,000 miles (386,000 km) from both the Earth and the Moon. In such a location, known as a Lagrangian point, the combined effects of the Moon's and the Earth's gravities lock any body placed in position there, preventing it from drifting away.

Space wheels and cylinders

Space colonies — huge cities that would float in deep space — are not such pie-in-the-sky ideas as one might think. As early as 1975 NASA initiated a study of possible designs for hardware to support a substantial space settlement. It was carried out at Stanford University and Ames Research Center in California, under the technical direction of Princeton's Gerard K. O'Neill, who had been working on space colony concepts for some years before.

Among the concepts considered, wheel-shaped and cylindrical habitats seemed to be the most feasible. The wheel design, known as the Stanford torus, would consist of a tube some 430-ft (130-meters) in diameter, forming a ring over 1-mile (1.6 km) across. This tube would form the main habitat and agricultural areas of the colony. Sunlight would be reflected into the tube via mirrors and louvers, which would be adjusted to control the internal 'climate'. Plants would be raised under ideal conditions, producing several crops a year. The sunlight would also be harnessed to generate electrical power for the colony.

Spokes would radiate inwards from the tubular habitat to a central hub, where there would be communications, docking, industrial and research

This space colony is of the so-called torus, or wheel-shaped design. The population of about 10,000 would live in the outer tube. The outer surface of the tube is coated with slag to provide shielding against the harmful cosmic radiation that permeates space. The slag would be a by-product from the processing of lunar ores into metals for the colony's construction.

modules. The whole wheel habitat would rotate once every minute, setting up centrifugal forces to simulate normal Earth-type gravity. For the 10,000 residents of the colony 'up' would be towards the central hub.

The equivalent cylindrical habitat design, also favored by O'Neill, would consist of pairs of cylinders 0.6-mile (1-km) long and 650-ft (200-meters) across. The land areas would run in three strips lengthwise around the inside of the cylinders. The strips in between would be glass, into which sunlight would be reflected by long hinged mirrors.

Above
When the time comes for planetary exploration, Mercury will not be a top candidate. Being the closest planet to the Sun, it is scorching hot. It has no atmosphere, and the surface is covered with craters, rather like the Moon.

This is another torus-type space base that features a huge solar power facility. It could well be used as a mammoth industrial complex that would supply materials and structures for large-scale space engineering works throughout the solar system.

For a long time thought to harbor life, Mars will be the first planet we shall visit some time in the next century. This view from Viking of the appropriately named Red Planet shows clouds formed near one of the planet's huge volcanoes, and frost in one of the great Martian basins. Both are evidence of an atmosphere. Some scientists reckon that in the distant past Mars had flowing water and a less extreme climate than it does now.

The surface of Mars, as viewed by one of the Viking landers. The rusty red color is probably caused by the presence in the soil of superoxides of iron. The sky is pinkish-orange due to the presence of fine surface dust kicked up by the surprisingly strong winds that whip across the planet.

To the Red Planet

Most probably before anything so exotic as the Stanford toruses or O'Neill cylinders are built, manned exploration of the planets will have started. Of the eight other planets in our solar system only the nearest ones, Venus and Mars, are close enough to contemplate visiting. And even these are respectively 26 million and 35 million miles (42 and 56 million km) away at their closest approach to Earth. In some respects Venus and Mars are the planets most similar to the Earth. Venus is a near twin of the Earth in size, and the Red Planet Mars has a day nearly the same length as ours and also has seasons. Both have atmospheres.

Until the coming of the space age, it was thought that both might, just might, support life of some sort. Now, thanks to visits by planetary probes, we know much better. Venus has a thick atmosphere of carbon dioxide at a pressure 100 times that of a atmospheric pressure on Earth. And the 'greenhouse' effect of this atmosphere pushes the temperature at the surface to beyond 840°F (450°C). Mars by contrast has a very thin

atmosphere, again mostly of carbon dioxide, and the temperature even at noon in midsummer on the equator scarcely rises above freezing point. Any form of life on Venus thus must clearly be absent. And the likelihood of life on Mars is also negligible. The Viking probes that landed on Mars in 1976 certainly found no signs of life, though they analyzed the soil. But they and the Viking orbiters showed a Mars so fascinating that it cries out to be explored. And so it will, some time in the future.

A Martian odyssey

The problems of sending a manned expedition to Mars seem almost insuperable with present-day technology. Even with the most favorable launch window, a round trip to the planet would last nearly two years. For most of that time astronauts would be traveling in zero-g. The effects on the human body of such prolonged weightlessness are unknown, although Russian cosmonauts have survived eight months of weightlessness with no apparent long-term effects. Even more unfathomable are the psychological effects of

We shall not be in a hurry to send manned missions to explore the outer solar system, where it is deathly cold and the planets are just balls of gas (mainly hydrogen). We shall leave exploration, as now, to robot space probes like Voyager, which sent back this picture of the beautiful ringed planet Saturn and three of its many moons.

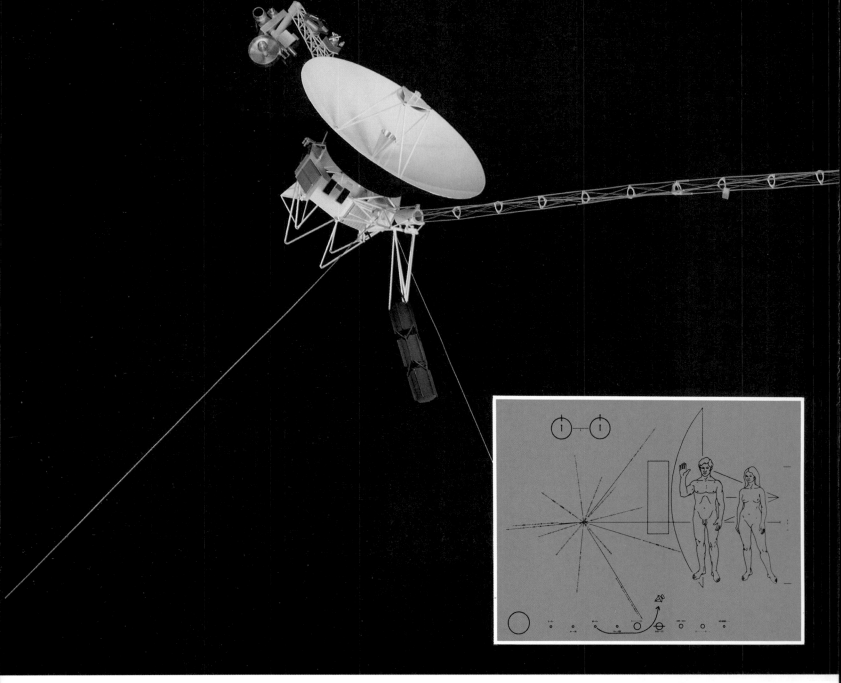

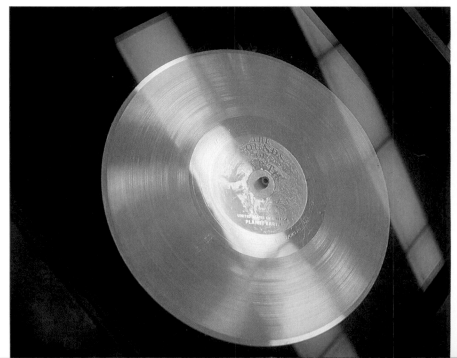

Above
The incredibly successful interplanetary probe Voyager 2, which has visited the planets Jupiter, Saturn and Uranus in turn, and is now on its way to Neptune. It will then leave our solar system and head for the stars.

Right
Each of the two Voyager probes is carrying a disc like this that contains electronically coded information which depicts the variety of life on Earth. It carries messages in sixty Earth languages and images that aliens should find fascinating!

116

Inset picture
A plaque like this is
carried by the Pioneer 10
and 11 probes, now
traveling through
interstellar space. Any
aliens that may find them
should be able to
discover where they
came from, from the
pictographs.

undertaking such a prolonged journey into the unknown with no hope of rescue in an emergency.

Despite the formidable problems a flight to Mars would present, NASA Administrator James Beggs has suggested (in July 1985) that the space agency's long-term goals should include a manned mission to Mars. Speaking on the tenth anniversary of the joint US/Soviet flight, the Apollo-Souyz Test Project (ASTP), he also floated the idea that a Martian odyssey should be another joint US/Soviet mission.

Craft quite different from today's Earth orbiters would be required for such an interplanetary voyage. Probably a new type of propulsion unit would be needed — perhaps a nuclear rocket engine, similar to one called NERVA (nuclear engine for rocket vehicle applications) which NASA test-fired in 1969. Indeed it featured in a mission to Mars study carried out by NASA about that time. The mission envisaged a manned landing on the planet in spring 1986, with a return home by the late fall.

Astronaut-gardeners

On such a long voyage it would probably be essential to recycle consumables like water and air. Waste water and urine would have to be reprocessed. Ideally, the crew would grow some of their own food in mini-greenhouses using hydroponic technology — raising plants in nutrient solutions rather than soil. The Russian cosmonauts already grow plants in miniature gardens in their Salyut space stations, apparently finding the experience therapeutic as well. (The idea of astronauts getting their relaxation by gardening is appealing!)

Among the other potential hazards of lengthy deep space flights, it is believed that solar flares could be the worst. Flares give out intense streams of radiation that could kill an unshielded astronaut instantly. So interplanetary space ships would need to be suitably shielded. One suggestion is to surround the crew quarters with water, which would act as a radiation shield. If the engines were nuclear, shielding would also be necessary to protect the crew from their radiation.

Terraforming

A more exotic way of spreading Man's influence throughout the solar system is by terraforming. This means reshaping a planet to a replica of the Earth. Venus is a prime candidate for this, of course, because it is so near the Earth in size. In order to terraform Venus two main things would

have to be done. To begin with the thick atmosphere of carbon dioxide, which exerts such a crushing pressure at the surface, must be replaced by a thinner one containing oxygen. And the temperature at the surface must be brought down from the lead-melting 842°F (450°C) it is at present.

An ingenious plan to do both at the same time has been suggested, which relies on some of the most primitive living things on Earth — blue-green algae. The scenario goes like this. Rocket-loads of algae would be injected into Venus's atmosphere, and start to feed voraciously on the carbon dioxide there, multiplying at an astronomical rate and giving off oxygen as they did so.

The atmosphere would slowly — over a period measured in centuries — become lighter and clearer. The 'greenhouse' effect would be so reduced that solar heat could escape through the atmosphere. The planet would slowly cool, and eventually water vapour in the atmosphere would condense and fall as rain, cooling the surface still further. In time Venus would turn into a vast humid swamp, and then the time would be ripe for human colonization to begin.

An even more bizarre scheme envisages bombarding the planet with asteroid chunks with such a force that the atmosphere is blasted into space. Self-replicating machines will then manufacture and erect a sunscreen to shield Venus from the Sun, and it will gradually cool. Later other self-replicating machines will process the surface rocks to liberate oxygen to form a breathable atmosphere.

To the stars

With only one foot, as it were, in interplanetary space at present it is perhaps pointless to speculate whether we shall ever journey beyond the solar system to other stars. Beyond the solar system, space is virtually empty out to a distance of some 25 million million miles (40 million million km). This is how far away the nearest star is, Proxima Centauri. Even its light, traveling at 186,000 miles (300,000 km) a second, takes over four years to reach us. So even a round trip at the speed of light would take over eight years. A conventional rocket setting out today on such a journey would take in excess of 100,000 years to complete it!

For interstellar travel to be feasible, revolutionary new means of propulsion will be needed. Several have been suggested, including photon rockets, which use intense beams of light as a means of propulsion; ramjets that scoop up

interstellar hydrogen and use it as fuel; and nuclear fusion rockets propelled by mini H-bomb explosions. And there have been many wilder notions of interstellar travel suggested, postulating such things as mysterious 'wormholes' through space that provide shortcuts across the galaxy and even to other galaxies!

Though we cannot ourselves yet make the journey to the stars, we can send robots there. The deep-space probes Pioneer and Voyager are already on their way. One day they could encounter other planets around other stars, and be recovered by other intelligent beings. Those extraterrestrials will then know, if they did not know it before, that they are not alone in the universe. For their further information, the Pioneers carry plaques that depict the kind of creatures who sent them and where in the galaxy they live. The Voyagers carry a record disc, which carries electronically sights and sounds of our civilization. Those extraterrestrials have a treat in store!

Above
In 1974 the giant radio telescope at Arecibo in Puerto Rico beamed a coded message into space telling about the nature of life on Earth — the genetic code, the molecules of life, the outline of a human being and its population on Earth. The message is still on its way. Will we one day receive a reply and know once and for all that we are not alone in the universe?

Right
Somewhere up among the stars there must be other planets on which conditions are very much like those on Earth. Do they possess life forms like those on our home planet? Perhaps we may never know.

Inset picture
Antennae much more powerful than the Arecibo dish will be needed if we are to establish communications with distant stars. This giant complex of antennae measuring some 10-miles (16-km) across might be the answer. Named Cyclops after the one-eyed giant in Greek mythology, it might even be able to beam signals to other galaxies, though we might have to wait for millions of years for a reply!

WATERLOO HIGH SCHOOL LIBRARY
1464 INDUSTRY RD.
ATWATER, OHIO 44201

Living in space   16790
Kerrod, Robin   629.47 Ker

Picture Credits

The majority of the photographs appearing in this book were provided by NASA through Spacecharts, to whom many thanks. Grateful thanks are also extended to the following individuals and organizations for providing additional pictures. (B = Bottom, T = Top, L = Left, R = Right)
Alabama Space and Rocket Center 23; **Arecibo Radio Observatory** 118; **Boeing Aerospace** 94/95, 104T; **British Interplanetary Society** 14B; **British Aerospace** 46B; **European Space Agency** 47; **Imax Systems Corp** © **Smithsonian Institution/Lockheed Corp** 52/53; **Robin Kerrod** 19B, 37, 38B, 41, 101B, 116B; **Novosti** 19T, 33, 82T, 87

Multimedia Publications (UK) Limited have endeavored to observe the legal requirements with regard to the suppliers of photographic material.

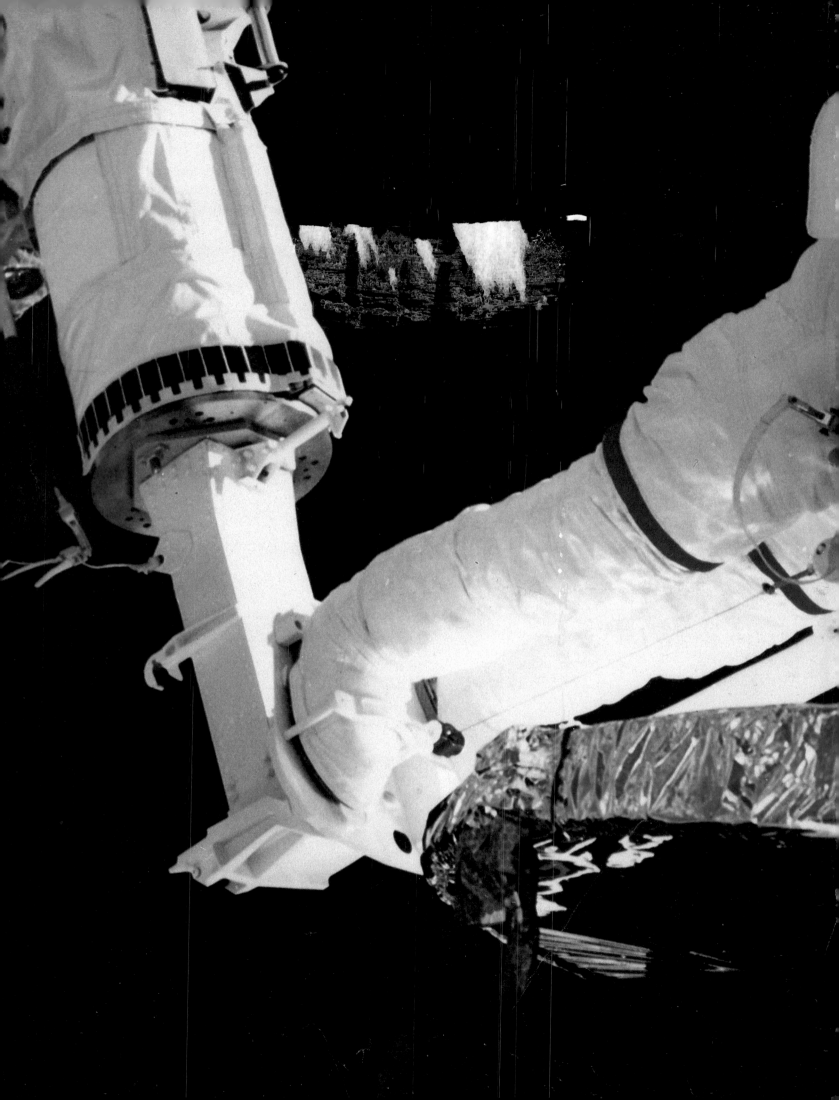

629.47
KER

629,47
Ker

Kerrod, Robin

Living in space

DATE DUE

DEMCO

629.47
KER